ONE NEW MAN

REUVEN DORON

foreword by Francis Frangipane

©1993 **Embrace**

Reuven Doron
River of Life Ministries
3801 Blairs Ferry Rd NE
Cedar Rapids, IA 52402

ISBN 0-9629049-9-6

Second printing, June 1996

In Memory of Rachel

This work is dedicated to the glory of God in memory of our daughter Rachel. This precious little seed was born February 15, 1991, and fell into the earth and died March 22, 1991, at five weeks of age. Her birth, her death and the circumstances surrounding her short life will forever testify to the sovereignty and awesome ways of God as He unfolds His prophetic word, fulfilling all of His promises to both Jew and Gentile.

Rachel fell as a soldier in battle. Her little life is forever and fully invested in the rich soil of God's prophetic work. Therefore, it is our assurance and our comfort that her resurrection is not only reserved for the day of the last trumpet blast, but the fragrance of her life is present in the hearts of God's people today.

Contents

A Note to the Reader

Some men have the future already in their spirits. They are the leaders who will guide us into the realities of tomorrow. Concerning the relationship of Israel and the church, I know of no one who can better lead us there than my friend Reuven Doron. If Reuven's words are signposts, his life and actions are a highway to the glorious grace awaiting the church and her ancient companion Israel.

In my years of knowing and walking with Reuven, he has demonstrated the character of the **one new man** of which he writes. His words are not merely theory or theological arguments floating unattached to his character and life. Reuven is Christ's man sent from Israel to the church, and when he returns to his native Israel, he will be Christ's man sent from the church to Israel.

In this book you will discover many answers concerning Israel. You will also find entry into spiritual places which, perhaps, you had not planned on visiting. A number of the cultural limitations which hinder us will be removed, and you will find yourself, in a fresh way, reunited into the commonwealth of Israel.

In today's world there is a horrible, violent process going on called "ethnic cleansing." It is not a new process; throughout history this was one of the ways conquering nations subdued their vanquished foes. In our century, this happened in Nazi Germany against the Jews and Gypsies; it occurred in Cambodia and, at the time of this writing, it continues in Yugoslavia.

As vicious and hellish as this genocide is, God has a pure "ethnic cleansing" that comes from Him. Through the grace of God, our ethnic backgrounds are cleansed from the ancestral sins and national reactions to other's sins. We are delivered from that which isolated us from other peoples. Our national pride is replaced by national repentance; our sins are accounted for and atoned.

Reuven is one who carries the grace of God to bring cleansing to both Israel and the church from their ancient, ethnic hostilities. The result of this holy cleansing will be God's **one new man**.

Francis Frangipane
Cedar Rapids, Iowa
April 1993

In the Beginning . . .

We live in unprecedented times. The unfolding of history in our century has been so remarkably fast, and at times shocking, as societies, nations and whole cultures have been shaped and reshaped in a single generation.

Not only have we witnessed the rise and fall of ideological and political empires, but also the coming forth of nearly 100 sovereign nations since World War II! For the first time in nearly nineteen hundred years, the world and the church of the Lord Jesus are faced with the phenomenon of a restored Israel. And as the social, political and strategic challenges surrounding Israel seem enormous, they are, nevertheless, small in comparison to the spiritual implications of her resurrection and her survival.

Most doctrinal errors are born when an overemphasis is placed on part of a truth rather than on the whole. It is like trying to put together a puzzle, attempting to decipher the overall design by looking into the many and varied pieces, while ignoring the picture on the box which alone provides the complete design. In the same way, insight into the mystery of Israel and the church can come only as we consider the "big picture," thus understanding God's overall design.

There is no greater "picture" than that of **"the summing up of all things in Christ, things in the heavens and things upon the earth"** (Eph 1:10). All things, ages and realities find their true essence in Christ alone and will come to their true fulfillment in Him only. Jesus is the beginning and the end of all things. He is the reason, the means and the purpose of all creations. Whatever is not **"from Him and through Him and to Him"** (Rom 11:36) is not real, but is merely a fleeting illusion.

Israel, the church and the destiny of the nations also have no reality apart from Christ. The resurrection of ethnic Israel in our century is not accidental. Indeed, the mystery of God in Christ, as it unfolds in these last days, encompasses the drama of His bride drawn from among the nations, and the national and spiritual resurrection of the people of Israel in their land.

And, as the Father is summing up all things in His Son, it is in His heart to bring forth at the closing of this age a most glorious demonstration of His new creation, the **"one new man"** (Eph 2:15).

This creation, which is neither Jew nor Gentile, but is derived from both, is taking on the very nature and life of the Son of God. Thus, in this ultimate display of both humility and unity, the full blessing of everlasting life will find its richest, most glorious and eternal expression (Ps 133).

According to scripture, the Lord has reserved a rich deposit of revelation, wisdom, vision and courage for the last generation of our age. It is our privilege and responsibility, therefore, to dig deep, seek hard and employ every grace given us to attain these virtues.

SECTION ONE:

The Beginning of Reconciliation

1

Apology

Before the church can come into a full understanding and appreciation of who ethnic Israel is, and before Israel can fully come into the embrace of Christ, there must be reconciliation between the two.

The fact is that both parties have failed the Lord and each other; they are in need of healing and restoration and must extend forgiveness in order to be forgiven. Just as the Jewish people, according to scripture, have defiled themselves and the land with uncleanness and unbelief, so has the church forsaken her foundational devotion to Christ and grazed for centuries in the fields of secular humanism and pharisaic doctrines.

However, as much as Israel's need for restitution and repentance is concerned, we find no clearer scriptural indictment than that breathed through the prophet Ezekiel as he prophesied of Israel's drama of failure and restoration.

Then the word of the Lord came to me saying, "Son of man, when the house of Israel was living in their own land, they defiled it by their ways and their deeds; their way before Me was like the uncleanness of a woman in her impurity. Therefore, I poured out My wrath on them for the blood which they had shed on the land, because they had defiled it with their idols.

"Also I scattered them among the nations, and they were dispersed throughout the lands. According to their ways and their deeds I judged them. When they came to the nations where they went, they profaned My holy name, because it was said of them, 'These are the people of the Lord; yet they have come out of His land.'

"But I had concern for My holy name, which the house of Israel had profaned among the nations where they went. Therefore, say to the house of Israel, 'Thus says the Lord God, "It is not for your sake, O house of Israel, that I am about to act, but for My holy name, which you have profaned among the nations where you went.

" ' "And I will vindicate the holiness of My great name which has been profaned among the nations, which you have profaned in their midst. Then the nations will know that I am the Lord," declares the Lord God, "when I prove Myself holy among you in their sight" ' " (Ez 36:16-23).

These words of Ezekiel's prophecy stand as a divine decree against my people Israel. We have defiled the land God gave us; we have become unclean. God's wrath justly came upon us, and when He scattered us among the nations in His righteous judgments, there too we often profaned His holy name.

Our very dispersion is a constant proof of God's verdict against us. The fact that Jewish people are born today in San Francisco, London and Rio de Janeiro, instead of in the land of promise, spells one thing only—God's promised and well-deserved chastisement!

We have forsaken His covenant, silenced His prophets, and smothered His Word with humanistic teachings. Truly, we have brought no glory to our God during the many years of our dispersion, yet He has faithfully sustained us and kept the testimony of Israel through millenniums filled with suffering and reproach.

Israel, the very nation chosen and fashioned to represent God to the world, has missed the mark. We have failed, and the only scriptural remedy for re-entering the graces of God and the fellowship of His saints is repentance.

Therefore, as an Israelite myself, Jewish by birth and a native of the land of Israel, I ask the forgiveness of the people of God for our failure.

It is my conviction that God is drawing Israel and the church into the most precious and glorious oneness of the **one new man** spoken of in scripture. Yet, for reconciliation to fully have its redeeming impact, both peoples must humble themselves and receive the forgiveness of one another and of God!

2

One New Man

The revelation of this united and perfected company of saints, the "one new man," though clearly expressed in the Lord's words and the apostolic writings, has nevertheless been kept to be fulfilled at the end of this age. Indeed, Jesus cried out on the cross, "It is finished!" (Jn 19:30) However, the consummation of His finished work was to cover the span of the whole of the Christian era, with great concentration of prophetic fulfillment at its very end. Thus, the reality of the **one new man** presses upon us these very days.

Paul, in his appeal to the Ephesian disciples to properly recognize their glorious position in Christ Jesus and their place in the body, placed a special emphasis on the term **one new man**. As we read in Ephesians, chapter 2, the apostle had to remind the Gentile disciples of their pagan heritage, stressing **"that you were at that time separate from Christ, excluded from the commonwealth of Israel, and strangers to the covenants of promise, having no hope and without God in the world"** (Eph 2:12).

However, though these disciples indeed emerged from such a hopeless background, the apostle comforts them with the truth that **"Now in Christ Jesus you who formerly were far off have been brought near by the blood of Christ"** (Eph 2:13). Paul continues to explain that God through Christ abolished the enmity between Jew and Gentile, broke down the dividing wall, and made both groups into one! In fact, the apostle introduces a brand new terminology in God's plan for man, as he identifies this new peoplehood of God as the **"one new man"** (Eph 2:15).

It is only by the cross of the Messiah that these two unreconcilable groups, who were locked in mortal animosity and conflict, were brought into one body. In fact, so profound is the unity of this new body of redeemed persons that the scripture testifies, **"through Him we both** [Jew and Gentile] **have our access in one Spirit to the Father"** (Eph 2:18), thus establishing this unity as spiritual in nature!

We understand that this miracle was brought about to fulfill a specific and very special desire in the Father's heart. Our God longs not simply to save many souls from eternal damnation, but to surround Himself eternally with a people of faith, vision and passion. Indeed, this newly acquired access to the Father by one Spirit, which is reserved for the **one new man** company, is clearly and scripturally attached to that purpose of God's household, His family and His eternal dwelling place.

As the scripture continues to unfold this marvelous revelation, Paul's choice of words enters a "construction mode." This "masterbuilder" describes the newly created race (drawn from both Jewish and Gentile heritage, yet growing into the likeness of Christ Himself) as "building material." He wrote to those same disciples that in the Lord Jesus **"the whole building, being fitted together is growing into a holy temple in the Lord"** (Eph 2:21).

This purpose, Paul proclaims, is that **"in** [Jesus] **you also are being built together into a dwelling of God in the Spirit"** (Eph 2:22). Our Lord desires not only to come to His people during **temporary** visitations, but to unite with us at the closing of this age in a **permanent** habitation! Thus, He is preparing a permanent dwelling place for Himself among the sons and daughters of men.

The drawing together of both Jew and Gentile into the **one new man** company is the harbinger of the age that is to come. It speaks of the consummation of the purpose of God, who promised Father Abraham both natural and spiritual seed (Gen 13:16, 15:5). As the spiritual and the natural seed of God's elect unite in Christ, so shall the spiritual and natural realms unite in unhindered flow of divine life. Free exchange of the substance of heaven will transpire between the heavenly and earthly realms as the gates between the spiritual and the physical dimensions open wide!

This ultimate and mutual humbling of both Jew and Gentile, laying aside those things that divide while being poured into God's new mold, will result in the ultimate exaltation and glory that is promised to characterize the completed house of the Lord!

How magnificent and wonderful our God is who kept the best until the end! This **house of the Lord**; this **dwelling of God in the Spirit**, will have as its building material God's best creation—His newest and His final one—the **one new man**. This creation embodies His very nature and life through the mediation of Christ; life that is indestructible and incorruptible, unable to fail!

The wonder of it all is that the quality and virtue which God produces in His **one new man** creation will be branded upon the fabric of both Jew and Gentile, woven together into perfect unity and centered upon Christ.

Truly, even as it required both Jew and Gentile to join together in crucifying the Lord, so it requires both Jew and Gentile to harmonize again, this time to bring about the full expression of His resurrection life. For surely, **"how good and how pleasant it is for brothers to dwell together in unity! . . . For there the Lord commanded the blessing—life forever"** (Ps 133:1,3).

3

The Root of All Divisions

As we prayerfully look into the unfolding drama of Israel, the maturing church, and the coming together of the two, we face, by necessity, the deepest, widest, and most ancient of schisms in the fabric of humanity. There has never been a more severe separation with such devastating results than the one between Jew and Gentile.

The schism that exists between these two peoples started as soon as God called Abraham and appointed him to become the father of a nation. This nation, according to God's Word, will be **"My own possession among all the peoples . . . a kingdom of priests and a holy nation"** (Ex 19:5-6). Thus, the very fabric of humanity was rent at that moment, as the Lord God separated unto Himself a people who would be different, somewhat exclusive, and set apart for a specific purpose. As is often the case, the setting apart of the one necessitates establishing distance from the others. Balaam, while prophesying over Israel by the Spirit of God, said, **"Behold, a people who dwells apart, and shall not be reckoned among the nations"**

(Num 23:9). Indeed, the nation of Israel was placed on a lonely path.

As we know from scripture, Abraham's call came immediately following the account of the tower of Babel. One might say that the Lord's choosing and fashioning of Israel was His antidote and remedy to the great calamity and ensuing judgments which stemmed from this rebellion. Even as humanity wholeheartedly united in this blasphemous purpose to **"build for ourselves a city, and a tower whose top will reach into heaven, and let us make for ourselves a name"** (Gen 11:4), God was preparing the cure! In the midst of global anarchy, as all humanity opposed God, denied His Lordship, and resisted His messengers, a nation was sovereignly created by grace for a work of grace.

However, as soon as Abraham was commanded by God to **"Go forth from your country, and from your relatives and from your father's house, to the land which I will show you"** (Gen 12:1), a deep split occurred in the human race. From Genesis, chapter 12, and on to the end of Malachi, we witness the specific and exclusive dealings of God with one nation only. This nation was the sole recipient of the revelation of God—His favor, His blessing, and His chastisement. All other nations, in fact the rest of the human race, could relate to and interact with the God of creation through the agency and the mediation of Israel alone.

The Schism Deepens

As the testimony of the Old Testament records God's dealings with the human race through one chosen nation, so the testimony of the New Testament clearly displays the expansion of the divine plan. The holy seed of God was planted in the earthen womb of Israel, and the Christ was born. As He, in turn, fell into the ground as seed and was raised again, the church was born! As it is written, **"God, after He spoke long ago to the fathers in the prophets in many portions and in many ways, in these last days has spoken to us in His Son"** (Heb 1:1-2). Indeed, the same Word, which in the past came through Moses, the prophets, and the seers of ancient Israel, now came clothed in human flesh to provide for the reconciliation of all men to God.

Israel served God's purpose for that time in bringing forth the Savior of the world, the Messiah. Indeed, as a bloody and exhausted womb rests after the birthing of a child, Israel was laid aside for a season. The people now in exile, the national life almost extinct, and the land trodden by strangers, Israel was "put on hold," and a new agency was birthed.

The church was now anointed and commissioned to carry the testimony of the Living God to all creation. Healing, forgiveness and divine acceptance were carried throughout the lost nations of a dying world, as the church declared and demonstrated the Kingdom of God. A new race was born—a race whose members carry the image of God. These men and women are fashioned not after the likeness of the first Adam who fell, introducing condemnation and death to humanity, but after the likeness of the second Adam who prevailed, establishing righteousness to all who believe.

However, the ancient schism between Jew and Gentile resulting from Israel's election was still not bridged. The deepest of all divisions, the one between Israel and the nations, worked its way into that new race of the redeemed, finding even more poisonous expressions within the new peoplehood of God. Indeed, until this very day, the body of Christ carries the painful marks of gaping wounds where members are not joined to one another, and life cannot flow.

While at the cross of Jesus complete reconciliation was accomplished, we do not yet experience the fulness of it. At the cross, man was not only reconciled to God, having our sin atoned for, but man was also reconciled to man and to creation, as all hostilities, rivalries and prejudices melt in the presence of God. However, we know and cannot hide from the tragic truth of disunity and lack of reconciliation throughout church history, as well as in this day.

It is not the existence of many streams, nor the variety of expressions, that grieve the heart of God; as it is written, **"There is a river whose STREAMS make glad the city of God"** (Ps 46:4, emphasis mine). Rather it is the lack of unity among them that holds back His pleasure and full endorsement. It is not because some carry different emphases or walk in diverse anointings, but it is the arrogance, the exclusivity, and the lack of brotherly love that turns the Father's face and favor from us.

Many are the schisms in the body of Christ today. Many are the divisions between churches, movements and denominations. Many are the obstacles to accomplishing that unity of Psalm 133 which alone attracts the fulness of divine blessing and fulfills the global promise of John 17:21.

And why? Perhaps because the deepest of schisms, the most ancient of divisions, have not yet been healed. And perhaps Paul, seeing the potential disintegration of the body of Christ into many separate, disjointed fragments (which surely took place), addressed the very root of the problem as he wrote to the Ephesian disciples.

One Family Under Heaven

Paul exhorts the church to recognize that since the heathen nations now have access through the gospel into the commonwealth of Israel, there should be no further division between Jew and Gentile. Paul strongly reminds the Gentile believers of their carnal and idolatrous lineage, then emphatically declares that, **"He Himself is our peace, who made both groups into one, and broke down the barrier of the dividing wall"** (Eph 2:14). By revelation, the apostle saw and clearly taught the reality of a united, harmonious people!

Continuing this revelation, the apostle unveils the mystery of the **"one new man"** (Eph 2:15), that new race which is destined to carry the presence of the risen Christ throughout our sick and dying world; that "company of the redeemed," which is made up of both Jew and Gentile alike, yet in itself is neither. Nevertheless, in spite of the apostolic exhortation, the schism remained.

So fractured and disjointed the body of Christ became in the early centuries of this era that it gave much room for idolatry and deception, plunging headlong into a thousand years of spiritual darkness. The Mediterranean Basin, the Middle East, and southeastern Europe, once steeped in the power and the glory of the early days of the gospel, now laid in spiritual slumber, as carnal religious institutions and heathen powers competed for control of the masses.

Centuries of reformations followed, dotted with numerous revivals to this very day when both Israel and the church are being restored, yet we still are faced with a deep division within the ranks of the church itself between Jewish and Gentile brethren.

Jewish believers tend to separate themselves from the "ordinary" Christian expressions and create an exclusive environment where the unique, historic and ethnic flavors can be preserved and expressed. Gentile churches, still influenced by pagan practices, often view with curiosity, mingled with contempt, these attempts of the Jewish brethren to experience and portray the life of God through traditional Jewish filters. Either way, the Jew is still isolated in a spiritual ghetto!

Whole Jewish communities were forced into physical ghettos in order to accentuate their distinctiveness and cut them off from the Gentile world. And tragically, within the church itself, we find spiritual ghettos which perpetuate division and separation. Thus, the schism remains, even among the redeemed!

When Paul wrote of the breaking down of **"the barrier of the dividing wall,"** he laid the sword of the Word with apostolic authority upon the root and the cause of all other divisions in the body. While the **one new man** company is in the heart of God's purpose, and since Jew and Gentile **must** together form this **one new man**, blending in humility and self-denial, it has become a major target for demonic assault.

As long as Jew and Gentile remain unreconciled in the truest and deepest meaning of Christian love and harmony, there will always be various divisions throughout the body of Christ! As long as we refrain from self-denial, and promote self-preservation rather than unity, there will always be legal right for the spirit of sectarianism to plague the church. And, indeed, how plagued we are!

Thus, the root of all divisions is hidden in the ancient soil of hostility that still exists between Jew and Gentile, between Israel and the nations. This cursed soil has produced nothing but thorns and thistles for millenniums, perpetuating and worsening the breakdown. But, by the Blood of Messiah even this soil can be cleansed. By the Word of God our minds can be changed, and by the Spirit of Heaven our hearts can be created anew.

The Lord is raising up a standard of unity in our generation. **Unity—not uniformity!** Prophetic voices from various ends of the Christian spectrum are sounding the same trumpet, calling God's people to join together and harmonize in a last great awakening.

Was it not the Lord's own prayer that **"they may all be one"**? (Jn 17:21) And did He not call us to be **"perfected in unity"** so that **"the world may know that Thou** [the Father] **didst send Me"**? (Jn 17:23) Indeed, it was because they did not discern the body rightly that many of the Corinthian disciples became weak and sick (1 Cor 11:29).

If we will not seek for, find and appropriate the grace to flow with other streams and movements, even as to blend Jewish and Gentile expressions, we will not taste of the full victory that was wrought on the cross. This victory is reserved for a united church, for a peaceful household, for the **one new man!**

Heal Our Land

As with most problems, true and lasting solutions will only come when we deal with the root issue. This principle of "healing at the root" clearly appeared as the sons of the prophets cried out to Elisha when the axe head fell into the River Jordan. Elisha's reply was **" 'Where did it fall?' And when he showed him the place, he cut off a stick, and threw it in there, and made the iron float"** (2 Kings 6:6). That which was lost was restored at the exact same spot where it sank!

The prophetic insight directed the search to the very place where the damage occurred, and **there** the power of God worked. Likewise, we will do well to search out the cause of all divisions and sectarian strongholds at the exact same spot the roots were first sunk, between Jew and Gentile, between Israel and the nations.

The Lord promises to give us both the wisdom and the strategy as we apply ourselves to this battle. And even as the presence of Jesus, symbolized by the tree Moses cast in, made the bitter waters of Marah sweet (Ex 15:25), so the presence of Jesus properly applied to the poisonous root of sectarianism will bring restoration and healing, turning that bitterness also to sweet.

Where did our axe head fall? Where did we lose it? When exactly and over what did the church begin to divide? Was it not over the arrogant contentions and deceptive ignorance as to who is first in the body, who is prominent, and whose position is higher before God? Was it not into the soil of Jewish stubbornness and Gentile arrogance that the seed of sectarianism was first sown, as both groups questioned and wrestled with their position and identity in the body?

Jewish pride and self-preservation on the one hand, coupled with Gentile insecurities and arrogance on the other, gave rise to Jewish exclusivity and Gentile "replacement" mentality which claims they are the only true Israel. Spreading deeper into the body of Christ, this root of division and sectarianism worked its way to disunite and break down the emerging fabric of the **one new man.**

Indeed, those who are of the prophetic and redeeming nature must apply both faith and labor toward the healing of that ancient schism, if we are to see the restoration and the coming together of the people of God. We can continue our labors and intercession, wrestling against the many manifestations of our disjointed condition, or we can go to the core of the issue and disarm the spirit of sectarianism right where it was originally planted—between Jew and Gentile!

Let's be Responsible

Being an Israeli Jew by birth and Christian by rebirth, I make this appeal to my brothers and sisters in the Lord. Bringing with me the weight of prophetic fulfillment of promises made to my people and the glorious expectation for what is yet ahead for the church, I challenge you with these words.

TO THE JEWISH BELIEVERS:

There is a place upon which the Jew can stand as a Jew and yet remain free from a sectarian attitude toward the rest of the church. We must repent of and renounce all prideful self-sufficiency and be ready to lay down all peripheral and unessential traditions. Our natural identity goes far deeper than those traditions. It is rooted with Abraham, the Hebrew who followed God in obedience, and with Israel, who wrestled with God and was broken and blessed. These are the fathers of our people, and their character and lives define our true ethnic identity.

The Jew must recognize that his highest call is to serve the nations of the world. This purpose necessitates an open heart and a generous attitude toward them. This was the call of Father

Abraham, and this is still our call in the Messiah Jesus. There is no better way to activate the treasure that is hidden deep within our souls and in our national consciousness than to offer it humbly to the church, coming as part of the church rather than as outsiders.

Until there is a harmony and oneness of both Jew and Gentile on the grass roots level of the church, with common worship, intercession and warfare, we shall remain shallow, maintaining impressive confession while attaining only limited power.

TO THE GENTILE BELIEVERS:

The time has come for the Gentile church to humbly recognize that God was not done with natural Israel in A.D. 70. Though Jerusalem was destroyed as prophesied, and the national life was historically snuffed out in A.D. 135 at the last Jewish revolt, God's hand still sustained the people. Century after century, throughout the most horrendous persecutions, continual tribulations, and constant hardships, the natural Jew survived. Driven from country to country with no place to rest, the exhausted and scattered nation stumbled into the twentieth century only to be herded into Hitler's death camps as the world silently watched. And yet, out of such death and destruction God brought resurrection life!

The church can no longer ignore the miracle that is taking place in the Middle East in our century: the return of the Jews to the ancient homeland; the supernatural birth of the state of Israel and the restoration of Jerusalem as capital; the miraculous protection that has kept this nation through her many wars; and the present wonder of the exodus from both Russia and Ethiopia! Only utter foolishness and arrogance will explain away these phenomena or ignore them as insignificant coincidences!

God spoke that when He gathers the remnant of His people from all the lands, "**He will lift up a standard for the nations, and will assemble the banished ones of Israel, and will gather the dispersed of Judah from the four corners of the earth**" (Is 11:12). The true interpretation of Israel's supernatural regathering is this: God is raising up a **standard** for the nations in order to draw their attention to Himself! And the nations, indeed, see and stumble over this standard while, amazingly, much of the church still ignores it!

God is not finished with the Jews. Rather, He kept them until the end of the age so that He may display both His mercy and awesome power as He restores them to the land and to Himself. **Thus, the Gentile church must repent of its prideful arrogance born of insecurities, and accept with love, respect and gratitude the prodigal son who is coming back home.**

Heeding the apostolic warning of Romans, chapter 11, where the apostle uses the metaphor of the olive tree, let us be very mindful, therefore, not to be **arrogant** toward the natural branches nor be **ignorant** of this mystery (Rom 11:18,25). Both arrogance and willful ignorance are sins to be reckoned with and be repented of so as to obtain the full measure of grace we need at this hour.

4

The Last Generation

As the dramatic and sweeping movement of God's hand upon the nations of the world continues to extract His harvest, and as we consider Israel's supernatural restoration, we must be very sure that our sense of timing is biblically correct. Are we really witnessing end-time dynamics? Is the **one new man** becoming reality, rather than merely a distant theological concept?

We recognize that down through the centuries spiritual "trends" of highs and lows in God's activity on the earth were oftentimes associated with end-time expectations. Some of the great revivals were thought to be the harvest at the end of the age; some of the darkest seasons of spiritual depravity and ignorance were considered the great apostasy, and many of the evil and influential personalities which manipulated empires and nations were often believed to be the Antichrist.

However, though these events and seasons definitely carried prophetic significance inasmuch as they portrayed the unfolding of

God's prophetic Word, one main ingredient was still missing from the puzzle. That ingredient was Israel!

It is written concerning the Lord's timing, **"Thou wilt arise and have compassion on Zion; for it is time to be gracious to her, for the appointed time has come"** (Ps 102:13). These words were spoken in the context of a heartrending prophetic prayer; a cry arose from a people whose **"days have been consumed in smoke,"** whose **"heart has been smitten like grass,"** and whose **"enemies have reproached [them] all day long . . . because of Thine indignation and Thy wrath"** (Ps 102:3-10).

Hearing Israel's cry in these scriptures, one cannot hide from the historical trauma which not only meant natural suffering, persecution and turmoil, but also points to the reason and the heart of it all. It was **"because of Thine indignation and Thy wrath"** that **"Thou has lifted me up and cast me away"** (Ps 102:10).

Indeed, this cry wells up from the wounded soul of Israel (even as Moses prophesied in Deuteronomy, chapters 28 and 29), yet not without hope. Because of the Lord's faithfulness and His great mercies, He has appointed a time to have compassion on Zion. It is, as we just read in Psalm 102, **"the appointed time."**

There is an appointed time for everything. Every birth, every death, and every event under the sun is recorded in heaven. There was an appointed time for each of the feasts of the Lord to be observed and celebrated. These feasts could not be observed at just any time—only at **the appointed time.**

There was a designated time for the Passover Lamb to be slain on that dreadful eve in Egypt, a specific time for the first fruits to be brought forth and presented before the Lord. The Lord Jesus Himself was born of a woman at the ordained time. His death, as well, could not have taken place at any other day and hour but at **the appointed time.** He also rose at **the appointed time,** just as the scriptures prophesied, fulfilling not only the Passover but also the Feast of First Fruits. The Spirit came at **the appointed time** upon the waiting disciples on the Day of Pentecost and, likewise, God has **an appointed time** to rebuild Zion!

Not only does the scripture speak of the Lord having compassion on Zion (Ps 102:13), for her appointed time has come, but it goes on to declare that **"the Lord has built up Zion; He has** appeared in His glory" (v 16). Indeed, the rebuilding of Zion clearly speaks of the prophetic hope of restoring the children of Israel back to the homeland one last time and back to their God. Yet, this rebuilding of Zion is intimately linked with God's appearance in His glory! In fact, He promises that as He re-establishes Israel in her land, and as He vindicates His holy name in her midst, there shall be a glorious demonstration of His power, His love, and His righteous judgments to all creation.

In Our Lifetime?

The timing of it all is given us in these words, **"This will be written for the generation to come; that a people yet to be created may praise the Lord"** (Ps 102:18). The phrase **"the generation to come"** in the original Hebrew text reads LEDOR AKHARON, the Hebrew expression for **the last generation!** This scripture, therefore, clearly indicates that the message concerning the rebuilding of Zion and the coming glory of God is written for the last generation of man! And, as incredible as it may seem, the revelation concerning the restoration of Israel with its actual fulfillment in human history found root only in our generation, after millenniums of obscurity.

But, what is a generation? Is it twenty-five, forty or seventy years? While opinions vary on this subject, consider this: A generation is the time-span between a father and his offspring. Abraham was one hundred years old at the time Isaac, the son of promise, was born; thus, we have a possibility that a biblical generation could stretch for one hundred years in the dynamics of redemption.

Additionally, in the context of God cutting a covenant with Abraham, we find Him saying, **"Know for certain that your descendants will be strangers in a land that is not theirs, where they will be enslaved and oppressed four hundred years. . . . then in the fourth generation they shall return here"** (Gen 15:13-16). Again, we find in God's own words that a generation equals one hundred years in terms of redemption, as it was the fourth generation that would return to the land after four hundred years! By these two witnesses, we suggest that it is biblically acceptable to view a generation as one hundred years.

Interestingly, this conclusion also harmonizes with the historical witness that ethnic Israel and the church have both been in the throes of restoration for most of our century. Indeed, our generation (our century), starting from the early days of the Zionistic restoration and the mighty revivals of the early Pentecostal movement, has been witnessing and participating in these end-time acts of God.

In fact, until the twentieth century very few Christians had an understanding of God's purpose for Israel. It is also a fact that prior to 1948 hardly any of the mainline Christian denominations publicly stated or believed that God would raise Israel again in fulfillment of scripture. Indeed, this message of Israel's restoration was truly written for **the last generation!**

Ours is the only generation that has witnessed the physical resurrection of Israel and thus could comprehend, believe and intercede for this miracle, as well as for the promised spiritual restoration. In this way the scripture will be fulfilled, **"that a people yet to be created may praise the Lord"**! (Ps 102:18)

5

The Identity
of the Church

The primary and eternal identity of the church is the Lord Jesus Christ Himself. He is our origin, our head, our leader, and our very life! The church's nature and destiny are embodied in the Son of God, and we have no substance apart from Him.

It is also true that the church was brought forth in a natural context, emerging out of a natural people at a given point in time. The scriptures testify to this, as we read of the early church which was chiefly Jewish, her background Hebraic, and her ethnic characteristics mostly Israelite.

Naturally speaking, the church, which stemmed from the seed of Jesus, the anointed one of God, sprouted and blossomed in the soil of Israel. Thus, the birthing of Christianity and its introduction into the world came through, and in the context of, the nation of Israel.

Indeed, the cultivated olive tree (Rom 11:24) was the foundation for the new growth. And, of course, one cannot forget the gospel writers, the apostles, and the early leaders of the church who were mostly Jewish. Truly, as much as her natural identity is concerned, the church of the Lord Jesus finds her roots in Israel.

As the Christian community comes to grips with God's truth concerning Israel and the implications of this truth, these words must be carefully considered: "**Therefore remember, that formerly you, the Gentiles in the flesh, who are called 'Uncircumcision' by the so-called 'Circumcision'. . . remember that you were at that time separate from Christ, excluded from the commonwealth of Israel, and strangers to the covenants of promise, having no hope and without God in the world**" (Eph 2:11-12). Indeed, at times the Word of God can be painfully direct and aggravating to our flesh.

In this context and by the authority of the Holy Spirit, the apostle reminds the disciples in Ephesus of their lineage. He was addressing a group of believers which was predominantly Gentile, and the Holy Spirit found it necessary to remind them of their earthly origin. The godless and heathen roots of these Gentile disciples offered them nothing more than a purposeless and empty existence. For the most part, their forefathers walked the earth entrapped in the lusts of their flesh nature, void of conscience and morality, as idol worship and demonic practices were their heritage.

Interestingly, the apostle identified the Gentile's tragedy as being both separate from Christ **and** excluded from the commonwealth of Israel, thus having no hope and no God! What the church claims as her "**new**" covenant is, in effect, her one and only covenant! This everlasting covenant God established with His Son is new only to the Jew who had an old covenant with God. For the Gentile believer this is the **only** covenant! Indeed, Jeremiah expressed this very clearly, saying, " **'Behold, days are coming,' declares the Lord, 'when I will make a NEW covenant with the house of Israel and the house of Judah ' "** (Jer 31:31, emphasis mine). Thus, the Gentile disciples through Christ are introduced into Israel's new and better covenant.

The Mystery

Paul continues his exhortation to the Ephesian disciples, saying, "**by revelation there was made known to me the mystery . . . that the Gentiles are fellow heirs and fellow members of the body, and fellow partakers of the promise in Christ Jesus through the gospel**" (Eph

3:3-6). He is saying, in effect, that God in His great mercies never intended to limit His graces and covenant to Israel alone, but made a way to invite and include the nations. Paul actually states that the gospel is not an end unto itself, rather it is **"through the gospel"** that the heathen nations of the world can be brought into the embrace of God in Christ as demonstrated in His covenant with Israel.

In saying that **"the Gentiles are fellow heirs . . . fellow members . . . and fellow partakers,"** we are given a very clear picture of these disciples being joined into an already existing reality. Through the gospel, they are now being joined to a people and a promise which pre-existed them; thus spiritually speaking, they join the common-wealth of Israel!

One People

The church was never meant to be isolated nor divorced from Israel. It was not called to replace, displace or be separated from her. Rather, the church was called into **"the commonwealth of Israel."** Christian believers from the nations not only have the right to spiritualize the promises God made to Israel in the natural, but they have, in fact, joined an existing body and entered into the benefits of an existing covenant!

The picture of the olive tree in Romans, chapter 11, ought to clarify and seal this mystery to every open-minded child of God. Once and for all, in this metaphor describing the peoplehood of God, we find only one tree! Jewish branches and Gentile branches both have their sustenance and fruitfulness in the same trunk and root system. God did not start a "replacement" olive tree! Obviously, He was satisfied with His original design and purpose. Jewish branches, Gentile branches, black branches, yellow branches—many wonderful branches—find, by faith, their place in God's one olive tree.

And still the apostolic admonition stands, as Paul addresses the Gentile disciples of Rome, saying, **"you, being a wild olive, were grafted in AMONG them [the Jews] and became partaker WITH them [the Jews] of the rich root of the olive tree, do not be arrogant . . . remember that it is not you who supports the root, but the root supports you . . . For if you were cut off from what is by nature a** wild olive tree [pagan roots], and were grafted contrary to nature into a cultivated olive tree [Israel], how much more shall these who are the natural branches [the Jews] be grafted into their OWN olive tree?" (Rom 11:17-24, emphasis mine)

Indeed, it is contrary to nature for wild, uncultivated branches to be grafted into a cultivated tree. In agriculture, grafting usually demands that a refined, fruit-bearing branch be grafted into a root system which is not necessarily fruit-producing, but strong. However, in this biblical parable the order is reversed, as unfruitful Gentile branches are grafted into rich Jewish roots. Thus, pagan idolatries are exchanged for the blessed reality and substance of the God of Israel.

There is no human explanation to such a mystery apart from these words, "Oh, the depth of the riches both of the wisdom and knowledge of God! How unsearchable are His judgments and unfathomable His ways!" (Rom 11:33) God's great mercies and compassion move Him to act contrary to nature, in ways that even reverse the order of His own creation, so that multitudes from the nations can find shelter in His love and fulfillment in His Kingdom. It truly is wonderful to dwell together, Jew and Gentile alike, in God's glorious olive tree. We need not waste ourselves in preoccupation with our separate earthly identities, but instead humble ourselves and accept with joy God's verdict. For, "through the gospel," we all are "fellow partakers of the promise in Christ Jesus" though, naturally and ethnically, after the flesh, we are different.

The Promise

In his address to the Galatian church, Paul again refers to that "promise" as a central theme that goes along with our salvation and destiny. "For all of you who were baptized into Christ have clothed yourselves with Christ. There is neither Jew nor Greek ... slave nor free man ... male nor female; for you are all one in Christ Jesus. And if you belong to Christ, then you are Abraham's offspring, heirs according to promise" (Gal 3:27-29).

What is this promise which embraces both Jew and Gentile? What is that blessed expectancy in which both partake of Christ

Jesus and labor together in God's purposes? What was this hopeful expectation that glowed so intensely in the apostle's bosom?

We find that the Gentile disciples are not only related to Father Abraham spiritually but, also, are heirs of the promise. Surely, he was speaking of the promise God gave Abraham—that by him **all** the nations of the world will be blessed through his seed! (Gen 12:3) This, indeed, was God's original intent—to redeem and to heal the nations of the world as He grafts them into His Kingdom. Spiritually speaking, through Christ the church was born into that very promise of being a blessing to the world!

That ancient promise has not been changed, rearranged or improved upon. It is still the same, and we who **"were baptized into Christ . . . are Abraham's offspring, heirs according to promise."** That which for so long rested solely in the bosom of ethnic Israel exploded through the gospel and became the inheritance of the redeemed. The mandate to be God's vessel and instrument of blessing and healing in the earth is no longer exclusive to one race, but is now shared by God's sons and daughters from every tribe, nation and tongue.

6

Destined
for Him

Reuven Doron's Testimony
(An Israeli Jew is Captured by God)

This testimony is but one indication as to the hour in which we live. It is the story of my own salvation, as the Lord revealed Himself to me, convicted me of sin, and reconciled me to Himself. This story illustrates, on a personal level, God's purpose and timing toward Israel, and also the duty and privilege of the church as she is to usher Israel back to God through intercession and love.

I am Jewish by heritage and Israeli by birth. My inner search and the Lord's drawing, though very personal and unique, are somewhat similar to the wooings and dealings of God with many other young Israelis whom the Lord has brought to Himself in recent years, as the last great ingathering unfolds.

"For as many as may be the promises of God, in Him they are yes; wherefore also by Him is our Amen to the glory of God through us" (2 Cor 1:20).

Family Heritage

Understanding that none of us live or die unto ourselves in limbo, separate from society, culture, and the molding pressures of one's own heritage, my personal experience with God is, therefore, inseparable from His calling on my people and my family. And, as I look back to the first generation of my kin in the land of Israel, I still draw much encouragement and inspiration as I see the hand of God upon them.

Both my grandfathers led their households from Russia to what was then called Palestine in the early years of this century. One came by boat while the other, after sending his wife and children over the sea, led a group of men on foot across the mountains of Turkey and into northern Galilee. Many incredible experiences were woven into their life stories as they traveled. Once they even disguised themselves as Christians while traveling aboard Russian trains to avoid the mounting persecution.

As both families were carried almost simultaneously upon the great wave of the Zionistic dream, settling in and investing their lives in the ancient homeland, my grandfathers left a deep mark on the emerging nation. In fact, their names are remembered and loved to these very days.

The one, who was an engineering and business genius, played a significant part in laying the industrial foundation for the young economy. The other, my father's father, became an influential personality in the early days of the Jewish underground movement. Radical and militant in character, he played an important role in the out-lawed campaign to secure the safety of Jewish communities from Arab hostilities during the oppressive years of the British Mandate.

Indeed, I continually find great joy in the knowledge that my grandparents and their children were unquestionably equipped, sent and used by God in the natural restoration of Israel. And I find much comfort and strength as I recognize God's hand upon my life as the grandson of these "giants" whom God called to serve Him in Israel's spiritual restoration!

My Search Begins

My personal quest for truth started as soon as I began to question the condition of my soul and the realities surrounding me following my "bar mitzvah" on my thirteenth birthday. High school years, though enveloped in the overall sense of idealistic well-being of a nation rebuilding itself, were for me an emotional and social disaster. Being the youngest of five children, I carved my own path in life and, although our family enjoyed loving relationships and a measure of stability and financial security, my encounter with the world outside was harsh and less secure.

The best way to describe this season of my life is to say that it was a time of mental and emotional battle; either I had the upper hand by controlling and using others, or they had the upper hand doing the same to me. Rock music, drugs and loose living flooded Israel from Western cultures during this "hippie era," and I was not left unscarred. The only worthwhile memories I have of that season are the many poems I penned—reflections of my melancholic and philosophical voyage, spinning a gloomy web of endless search and frustration.

The army service provided relief from that futility of mind and soul. At eighteen years of age I joined a specialized military unit and decided to make something worthwhile of my life. The fact is that every Israeli, deep inside, no matter how frustrated or lost, really loves the land and the nation of Israel. And this mandatory army service is an excellent opportunity for young men and women to come to grips with the more noble side of themselves as they engage in sacrificial service to their nation.

Twelve months of rigorous combat training—physical, mental and technical—made men out of boys! Half of the hundred and twenty who volunteered for that unit did not withstand the testing and stress, while the sixty of us who graduated with honor entered into the legacy of this admired group. It was but a few days later that we were urgently dispatched to the northern border of Israel on the Golan Heights in light of intelligence reports concerning Syrian military buildup. Within 24 hours, hardly prepared, the armored division we were attached to, as well as the rest of Israel, were shockingly thrust into the "Yom Kippur War" of 1973 on the Day of Atonement.

Much has been written regarding this traumatic war. It will suffice to say, in this context, that during that time the Lord's hand fell heavily upon Israel with severity and chastisement, judging the prideful self-sufficient attitude that had resulted from the miraculous victory of the "Six-Day War" of 1967. As the armed forces were virtually caught unprepared in October of 1973, Israel was almost devastated. Heavy fighting ensued on all fronts simultaneously, and if even one battle had been lost, the whole war would have been over within a matter of hours, and Israel would have been flooded with murderous, hostile forces.

Yet, the Lord knows our frame, that we are but dust, and in every temptation He does provide a way of escape! His deliverance and miraculous help were again extended (not a moment too soon), and Israel, though victorious, was left to lick her physical and emotional wounds. So was I!

Time and time again, my life was miraculously spared in battle over the hills of the Golan Heights. Close friends and comrades were hit, blown apart and killed on my right and on my left, while I was merely scratched and lightly singed. One miracle followed another as one day of anxious and exhaustive fighting followed another, and the unexplainable phenomena of my survival became more and more undeniable and troubling to me.

Two-thirds of the men in my unit were left behind on the battle-fields, and much of my soul was left there with them. For years to come I was to carry the burden of dozens of dead comrades in my bosom—my private hell—ever alive and ever so painful!

For me, the war proved to be an encounter with realities of life and death for which I had no explanation. Questions faced me for which I had no answers. As a nineteen-year-old, though highly trained, the suffering and the loss I witnessed and experienced were absolutely void of any logic, reason or purpose. And being the kind of person that I was, these frustrating, unresolved, painful and shameful memories were nearly unbearable. Though it was years before answers came, this war—this encounter with life, death, suffering, and the unrestrained evil of the human heart—put me on the searcher's path more than ever.

Still, Life Goes On

It wasn't but a week after my discharge from military service that I had my backpack loaded and was on my way to the "great big world." At the time, getting out of the Israeli pressure-cooker and "relaxing" in the cradling arms of the prosperous and soft societies of the West was very tempting. Across Europe, through Canada, down to the United States, and on to Central America, my search drove me. Many miles, many months, many faces, and many places offered no comfort for my soul. On the contrary, the more I sought, the more I touched and tasted, the bigger the questions became. Yet, I found no answers! All I found were more troubled, confused and hurting people who also were looking for answers. Empty-handed and disillusioned, I returned to Israel.

A brief season of business activity in my father's firm, though lucrative, proved to be unsatisfying and premature for me. I left Israel again, this time to study. Although Israel offers some of the better higher-education institutions, I felt I must get out. Providence brought me to Phoenix, Arizona, where I enrolled in the Business College at Arizona State University. And though there were a number of natural reasons for my choosing that city, the reason of reasons was still hidden from my understanding.

After the initial cultural, social, and linguistic shock, I began to break into the subculture of campus life. This "tall and dark stranger" began to find his way through the maze of confusion, perversity, and lawlessness of the American college lifestyle. And since studies came easily for me due to the high standard of the Israeli educational system to which I was accustomed, there was plenty of time for me to get into trouble.

While I appeared successful, my inner life was deteriorating fast! The downward spiral of loose living and self-deception was beginning to get to me as I lost, one by one, the principles of life, reason and sanity I once cherished. I remember a point in time when I could no longer face myself in the mirror. Though I could successfully live a lie for everyone around me and deceive the whole world, I couldn't look into my own eyes! Deep down, beneath the heap of my corrupt flesh, genuine shame and remorse glowed in the darkness of my soul, like fading coals beneath the ashes of my life. Now desperate, my heart disillusioned with the pleasures of this

world—I was ready! And into this heavy heart came the Word of
God!

In fact, His Word had come to me three years earlier while
partying on the streets of New Orleans during the Mardi Gras with
thousands of other disillusioned, lost and hurting souls. A street
preacher spotted me and, with love, began to share the gospel. He
soon discovered that I was from Israel and, with the overly zealous
reaction of one who loves Israel and the Jewish people, fell on my
neck, hugging and kissing me as if finding his long-lost brother.

That did it! Even if I could mockingly endure his "spiritual bab-
bling," I absolutely had no stomach for the hugging and the kissing
business. I pushed him from me and walked away. Rejecting him on
that day, I also rejected the outstretched arm of the Lord. This
remained the condition of my soul until I found myself in Phoenix,
Arizona, three years later.

"One Jew, Lord;
One Jew For Your Kingdom . . ."

A divine appointment led me into a supernatural friendship with
a man whom otherwise I would never have met. Our relationship
was based on business, as I gave him private lessons in the Hebrew
language, one of the part-time occupations I held at the time.

However, it didn't take long for me to realize that I was dealing
with a unique personality. Though outwardly a very average middle-
class American, inwardly Frank was different. And, it wasn't but a
few weeks into our Hebrew lessons that it dawned on me that he
was not Jewish! The fact was that all the other Hebrew students I
tutored at the time were very much Jewish, and having a blue-eyed,
blond-haired Hebrew student of Scottish descent was quite unusual!

This Christian man understood God's plan for the Jewish
people. By revelation he knew it was time for the veil to be removed
from many Jewish eyes and for a harvest of Jewish souls to pour into
the barns of God. However, he didn't set about to start a Messianic
congregation; neither did he establish a mission for the Jews.
Rather, he started to pray!

For years he lifted this prayer up to the Lord: "**One Jew, Lord;** one Jew to come into your Kingdom. Keep him, Lord. Protect him and bring him to me; prepare him for your Word. **One Jew, Lord.**"

In fact, my new friend was so intent on finding this one Jew for which he had prayed so long, that he took no chances. He committed before the Lord not to initiate any spiritual conversation with me unless the Lord would prove to him that I was that man. And so he prayed again, saying, "If he is that man, if You brought him to my doorstep (as the Lord had truly done), then make him ask me the right questions. Prove to me that he is the one."

And sure enough, before long I began to ask questions. "Why would you, a blond, blue-eyed Gentile, ever desire to learn and speak the Hebrew language?" To this question my newly found friend answered, "My heart's desire is to be able to read the scriptures in the original Hebrew language." At his response I laughed so hard that my eyes filled with tears. "The Bible?" I said, "Why would you want to read the Bible in Hebrew? What is in it, anyway?"

You see, I thought I knew the contents of the Bible. After all, in Israel we studied this book for many years in both elementary and high school classes. I was certain there was nothing in that book but ancient legends and national myths; the Jewish answer to Greek mythology! The God of the Bible seemed very impersonal and distant; the miracles recorded were to me but natural phenomenon which could be scientifically explained and reproduced; the prophets, kings and warriors were merely charismatic personalities, and the standard of morality and holiness was no more than Jewish uniqueness in the face of universal paganism. "So, what is in the Bible anyway?" I asked.

His answer, this time, brought no laughter nor mockery from my lips. "In the Bible," he said, "I find the knowledge of the **living God!**" Twenty-four years of search, frustration, and near-despair came to a screeching halt! The living God? Is there a living God? Can He be alive for me?

Needless to say, life was never the same from this point on. Our Tuesday and Thursday evening sessions, which were to end at 10:00 P.M., stretched deep into the nights as we searched the scriptures together. We studied the account of creation, the patriarchs, the exodus from Egypt, the judges, the kings and the prophets. We looked into issues of life and death, heaven and hell, and blessings and curses, learning of the promised Messiah. And while these studies were quite basic, my soul was being cleansed bit by bit, my heart claimed inch by inch, by the very Word of God.

Life in the world became worse than ever as conflicts and frustration intensified. My inner reality was being changed and transformed daily. I was not a "good sinner" anymore. I became a "miserable sinner," as I now was under increasing conviction. The revelation of the Living God grew closer and clearer, upsetting all the little gods that enslaved me. They screamed in terror, yanking at my rotting flesh in desperate attempts to keep me bound in their traps—but without success! It was Jesus Himself who promised concerning His followers that, **"No one shall snatch them out of My hand. My Father, who has given them to Me, is greater than all; and no one is able to snatch them out of the Father's hand. I and the Father are one"** (Jn 10:28-30). And though ignorant of this promise at the time, I was being carried on its wings.

A few more weeks elapsed into our studies in the Word, and I found I could not live in both worlds and maintain my sanity any longer. My college studies faded into an insignificant blur of futile mental gymnastics, my friends seemed more like enemies, and the world itself encroached upon me as a dark oppressive cloud. The only way out was by that narrow gate through which I could already see the light. Distant and faint as it was, this light was very real. In fact, it was quickly becoming the only light for me.

I did not know who God was nor was I acquainted with His ways, but this I knew—I had to find Him out! Frustrated and pushed by the deteriorating circumstances of my life, I told my God-sent friend, **"If there is a God, if He is alive and caring and interested in me, if He really paid for all my sin and misery, I do not want to only read about Him or just hear of Him—I need to know Him!"**

My friend, who understood the moving of the Spirit in my heart, simply said, "Go pray. Seek His face." This simple challenge exposed an absolutely undeveloped region of my soul. Pray? Seek God? How do you do that? Does God speak Hebrew or English? Do I need to kneel or stand? Will He smite me if I say the wrong words? Is He even listening? Is He there?

Wrestling With God

With all these questions and more, I entered a season of seeking God intensely. Late in the nights, after I was done with my daily routine of school, work, social life and jogging, I began to talk to God. All alone, kneeling upon the tall grass in my backyard, I began to address this mysterious, invisible God. I wasn't sure He was there. I wasn't sure He was listening. But I had to find Him out.

Since I had no religious upbringing nor any traditions to rely upon, I had to quickly create my own. I reasoned that God must know everything since He made all things; therefore, I began to ask Him many questions. Difficult questions. If He really wanted to reveal Himself to me, He could certainly do it by providing answers that I could in no other way find, and thus I would have proof of His existence.

And so, I asked. Many questions crossed my lips during those long nights: questions pertaining to the history of the world and of the universe; questions concerning this present age, its philosophical foundations, and its tragedies; questions concerning me, my family, friends, and other unresolved, dead-end realities which choked my soul.

Hour after hour, night after night, I poured out my heart. Yet the heavens were silent. God sent no message, commissioned no angel, and uttered no word. He remained cloaked in distant, silent garments. What I did hear, loud and clear, was the voice of the adversary. The Accuser of the Brethren was constantly pouring out accusations and deceptions, attempting to flood over my soul with discouragement and confusion. His whispers could almost be picked up audibly as he laid into me: "Stop praying! Shut up! No one loves you! No one listens to you! No one will answer your foolish questions! Go home! Get back into your warm bed lest the neighbors hear you talking to yourself and ship you back to Israel as a madman! Stop praying! There is no one out there!"

As all accusations and deceptions are intended to produce, these too began to form a thick and dark barrier around my mind that I had to break through. And I did—not because I was virtuous or wise, but I was so desperate! For the first time in my life I was drawing near to something solid and secure. For the first time I found a foundation that I could possibly build my life upon, and I was not about to give it up easily. If there was such a wonderful and awesome God as the scripture portrayed Him to be, I had to find Him out. If He was real, my life would be His. If He was false, I would go back into the world and live like a devil because it wouldn't mean a thing anyway!

My questioning God lasted only for so long. At a very late hour during one of those nights of searching, I came to the end of myself; I had no more questions to ask, no more mysteries to unravel—yet the heavens were still silent. In that deafening silence, in that great emptiness of mind and soul, I came upon a great discovery. It dawned on me that, though not raised in an Orthodox Jewish home, I had still set myself to seek the Living God the way an Orthodox Jew would do.

In my heart I reasoned that if I could prove that God exists—the God of Israel, the creator of heaven and earth, the one and only God—only then, after finding Him, would I consider Jesus. Only after connecting with the Father would I examine the claims of the Son. Yet God, who looks to the heart and is not impressed with our many words, didn't even "wink" in my direction! As long as I did not acknowledge my need for a savior, God kept His silence! Truly I was living out the reality of the scripture that says, **"Whoever denies the Son does not have the Father; the one who confesses the Son has the Father also"** (1 Jn 2:23).

Captured!

All alone in that late hour of the night, that late hour of my life, far away from home, I counted the cost. Truly, Jesus is indeed a major stumbling block for a Jewish person. The veil upon our hearts is truly thick and is even made thicker by the tragic atrocities we have suffered for centuries at the hands of Christians. But now I knew I needed a savior! Now I was beginning to understand that there is no way to be reconciled to the Father without one.

And so, I offered up the last question I found in my soul—that question which was hidden deep beneath the pile of mental and philosophical garbage that first had to be spewed out. From deep within me welled up a cry that reached the heavens. This one came, not from a calculating and manipulating mind, but born from desperate need, deep conviction, and an intense longing for the living, loving God. I could not escape any longer from asking that one last question: "Do I need Him? Do I need the Nazarene in order to come to You?" This question came with genuine anger and frustration. I felt cornered by God. Trapped between my need and His love, I had no way of escape.

This time, God answered! Out of heaven came an arrow of revelation piercing through the darkness of the night, the world, and my soul. His Word now sparked my spirit alive with a blaze of truth as He spoke, "Yes" and "Amen! You need the Nazarene!"

For the first time in my life, I consciously heard God. The ring of His Word was so clear and loud that, even if the word had come audibly, the sound would have been insignificant compared to the thunder in my spirit! And so I stayed right there, kneeling in my backyard, drinking in the life and nectar of His Word.

I wasn't "slain in the Spirit," nor was I aware of a legion of angels dancing over my head in celebration. Rather I remained very still, aware only of His presence. I was listening to the echo of His voice ringing through the chambers of my heart, washing, cleansing and healing as it permeated my soul.

It was some time before I stood to my feet and returned to my apartment. To my amazement, a most unusual sensation and realization came upon me. I remember saying to myself, "Reuven, you have changed. You need to get reacquainted with yourself." You see, though I had no intellectual knowledge of the new birth doctrine, I simply was spiritually "born again" as the seed of heaven was planted in my heart! Neither was I acquainted, at the time, with the scripture from 1 Corinthians 1:20, which declares that all of God's promises toward us are "yes" in Christ, and our "amen" toward God is through Christ as well. Yet, these were the very "rhema words" God spoke into my spirit that night to establish Jesus as mediator between the Father and myself. Yes and Amen! You need the Nazarene!

Life took a radical turn. I was immediately thrust into the most beautiful yet painful season of my life, as much of "me" was crucified and a "new creation" was being birthed. Friends and relationships vanished out of my life; bridges were burned overnight. I was quickly, almost violently, stripped of my worldly garments and gently covered with heavenly ones. The circumcision of Christ that is done without human hands cut through the fabric of my very being. New people now appeared in my life—not those of my choosing—but of the Father's. And after six months of such wonderful and terrible dealings, the Word of the Lord came to me again saying, "Go home, son. You are now ready!"

Returning to Old Battlefields

It was time to return to the land of Israel. I knew God wasn't finished at all with the process of maturing and perfecting my soul, but rather had brought me to a place where I could now endure the cup of spiritual assault and testing which would soon be mine to drink. And so it was.

My family, friends and army comrades seemed to be commissioned from heaven to test my faith, hope and love. For the next few years I was to endure constant rejection, suspicion and isolation from the ones I loved the most. Rabbinical squads were sent to me for the purpose of destroying my new-found faith, seeking to undermine the reality of the risen Messiah and deprogram my soul! These were years of sweet suffering, where only the nearness of the Lord kept my heart from breaking.

Yet simultaneously, to balance all that battle, there was the young and precious body of believers, most of them "first fruits" like myself, assembling together to discover and obey the calling of the Lord. We had very few teachers and traditions to fall back on. We were the generation which was to see the beginning of the restoration of a living, loving church in the national frame of a restored Israel after centuries of absence and void.

Love and faith, being more powerful than hatred and fear, conquered. Within a few years of struggle and intense prayer, my whole family began softening before the love of God, giving increasing consideration to His Word. The Spirit of God gained impact as conviction and hope welled up together in their hearts. By now, they all are in various places of response to God's saving grace and to His presence. And as these battles were being won, the Lord's plan and purpose for my life unfolded as well.

Years of maturing and ministry followed, during which I served in various ways within the emerging body of Messiah in Israel. We were privileged to see and to participate in the birthing of congregations throughout the country, bringing together nationwide gatherings of disciples, and unifying the spiritual leadership in the nation. Indeed, we were discovering and re-establishing the eternal truth that the church of Jesus not only was born in the context of the nation of Israel, but will also be gloriously revived and fulfilled in that same context at the closing of this age.

Presently, while we are serving in the United States for a season, we still believe that Israel will be carried into her spiritual fulfillment by the prayers, sacrifice and love of the Christians, and to that end we also labor. The church herself will not come into her own fulfillment without the spiritual rebirth and restoration of the natural branches of God's one olive tree (Rom 11:24).

SECTION TWO:

The
Story
of
a Nation

7

The First
of Nations

The nation of Israel emerged upon the scene of humanity
following the disastrous humanistic attempt to supplant God at the
Tower of Babel. Here, the entire human race joined in a united
rebellion against God, attempting to achieve spirituality and divinity
by man's own works! Under God's judgment, the human family
scattered in different directions. They now spoke different languages,
developed diverse cultures, and splintered into exclusive and hostile
ethnic groups. God, however, was already preparing the antidote!

Father Abraham, of whose loins came the nation of Israel, was
now called into the purposes of God and placed on His center stage.
A nation was born from him, through the patriarchs, that was not
the product of God's judgments, as all the other nations were, or the
will of man. Through this one nation God's remedy for the sickness
of the human race would come.

And while there was a kind and merciful plan in the heart of
God for all the nations, the nation of Israel was first: first to learn

of faith and obedience; first to experience corporate worship; first to have the Lord fight their battles; first to receive prophetic guidance and direction; first to be chastised and disciplined; first to possess the gates of their enemies and first to fall upon God's great mercies and unfailing love.

To the Jew first was granted the revelation of God and the Messiah. To the Jew first were entrusted the principles and ordinances of God's theocratic rule in a practical fashion. This holy realm and its moral principles could now be implemented on earth. And though only a shadow of the real substance, these principles now influence and guide the development of all God's children, aiming toward the final culmination in the incarnation of the Son of God.

For over two thousand years the Jewish nation was the only nation subject to God's moral code, His prophets, His chastisement, and His direct compassion. It appears from Old Testament accounts that God's dealings with other nations were related to His purposes to either punish or reward His **first-born nation.** Consider Cyrus, who was greatly blessed and used of God in the Jewish return from Babylon, of whom the scripture says, **"For the sake of Jacob My servant, and Israel My chosen one, I have also called you by your name; I have given you a title of honor though you have not known Me"** (Is 45:4).

And yet, we know that **God is love,** and even during this season of exclusive dealings with Israel His mercies were undoubtedly kindled toward the lost mass of humanity. As it is written, **"The Lord is good to all, and His mercies are over all His works"** (Ps 145:9).

Nevertheless, we cannot deny the clarity and simplicity with which the scriptural account testifies to Israel's unique standing before God. Indeed, as the apostle writes by the inspiration of the Holy Spirit, they **"are Israelites, to whom belongs the adoption as sons and the glory and the covenants and the giving of the Law and the temple service and the promises, whose are the fathers, and from whom is the Christ according to the flesh, who is over all, God blessed forever. Amen"** (Rom 9:4-5).

Could Paul really mean all that? Were all these awesome declarations necessary? For while we acknowledge that historically the Jewish nation was the first of the nations before God, Paul goes much further. According to his emphatic declaration, the **sonship**, the **glory**, the **covenants** (old and new), the **worship**, and the **promises** still "**belong**" to Israel. The language used is in the present tense and does not at all suggest something that is past and gone. Thus, imbedded deep within the ancient and weary form of the Jewish nation is a glorious seed that is yet to sprout and blossom one last time.

To the Jew First

Indeed, this is the apostle's proclamation, "**For I am not ashamed of the gospel, for it is the power of God for salvation to everyone who believes, to the Jew first and also to the Greek**" (Rom 1:16).

Looking at this often-used verse, we are reminded of and confronted with the fact that, scripturally, there is a revealed order in God's advancements toward man, as He draws closer and closer, age by age. Concerning the advent of the Son of God and the spreading of the gospel, the scriptures are very clear that it was "**to the Jew first.**"

In what way, then, is the Jew first? First in line? First-born? First chronologically or first place? How is the Jew first before a God who testifies concerning Himself that He is no respecter of men? How can any race be favored above others before a God who says that, "**all flesh is grass, and all its loveliness is like the flower of the field . . . The grass withers, the flower fades, but the word of our God stands forever**" (Is 40:6-8). Indeed, "**all**" flesh is like grass; temporary, frail and passing away.

The flesh alone, that earthly and carnal aspect of our make-up, avails nothing. Within itself, it possesses no virtue and contains no promise for our destiny with God. "**All**" flesh will fade away apart from the power and virtue of the "**word of our God**" incorporated into our lives, cleansing, sanctifying, and regenerating. Therefore, since we have no confidence in the flesh or its boastings, we focus on the promise of God and on His Word. Yet, we must wrestle with and come to understand God's declaration, "**to the Jew first.**"

As a second witness to this same point, we read, **"There will be tribulation and distress for every soul of man who does evil, of the Jew first and also of the Greek"** (Rom 2:9). Indeed, the scripture testifies that the Jew was not only first as far as the gospel and its power to save is concerned, but also first in tribulation and distress. From God's point of view the Jew appears to be first in both blessings and curses.

As Paul continues his writing to the Roman disciples, he follows with this: **"glory and honor and peace to every man who does good, to the Jew first and also to the Greek"** (Rom 2:10). It is clear, therefore, that the Jewish significance in this context is not rooted in greater importance, higher status or a more favorable position, but is directly related to the simple order and progression of God's dealings with man.

Scripturally, we find that the work of God in the context of the Jewish nation is a forerunner, a preparation, and a commencement for the rest of His works among the nations. Thus, **"to the Jew first"** could be understood in a chronological sense that is both historically proven and scripturally correct.

However, we must also make room in our hearts for the fact that Israel is first-born among the nations, a position that cannot be claimed by anyone else. For biblically, the first-born in the family not only was more privileged than the rest of the brethren, but also shouldered a heavier burden and responsibility.

In the context of Amos' prophecy of judgment against Israel, we find that the Lord's case against her is built on this exact premise: **"You only have I chosen among all the families of the earth; therefore, I will punish you for all your iniquities"** (Amos 3:2).

That uniqueness and precedence of call and destiny confronts us again in Jeremiah's prophecy. This time the Lord speaks of the restoration and regathering of Israel, saying, **"I will make them walk by streams of water, on a straight path in which they shall not stumble; for I am a father to Israel, and Ephraim is My first-born"** (Jer 31:9). Indeed, we must humbly accept the divine decree that Israel, the Jewish nation, is God's first-born among the nations.

Israel's Calling

Both the national existence of Israel and her calling find their origin in Genesis, chapter 12. **"Now the Lord said to Abram, 'Go forth from your country, and from your relatives and from your father's house, to the land which I will show you; and I will make you a great nation, and I will bless you, and make your name great; and so you shall be a blessing; and I will bless those who bless you, and the one who curses you I will curse. And in you all the families of the earth shall be blessed' "** (Gen 12:1-3).

While Abram appears to be a passive party to this covenant, God assumes full responsibility for the carrying out of these promises. The Lord continually says, **"I will make . . . I will bless . . . I will curse . . . "** This is His initiative, His plan, and He is fully committed to carrying it out on behalf of all the families of the earth! The nation that was to come out of Abram's loins, and which was spoken of prophetically in this scripture, was to carry a global calling. Israel was not only to be **"a great nation"** with limited territorial destiny, but rather **"you shall be a blessing . . . and in you all the families of the earth shall be blessed."**

From a New Testament perspective we find this revelation: **"And the Scripture, foreseeing that God would justify the Gentiles by faith, preached the gospel beforehand to Abraham, saying, 'All the nations shall be blessed in you.' So then those who are of faith are blessed with Abraham, the believer"** (Gal 3:8-9). Indeed, not only does the scripture testify that **"the gospel,"** the revelation of the "good news," was made known to Abraham, but also that God chose, fashioned, and equipped him to be, in turn, a blessing to all the nations of the world.

God's purpose was never limited to one nation only, nor was Israel selected as the sole beneficiary of His graces. **"For the promise to Abraham or to his descendants that he would be HEIR OF THE WORLD was not through the Law, but through the righteousness of faith"** (Rom 4:13, emphasis mine). That which was invested in Abraham's loins and spirit was not only for himself or for the nation he would bring forth; neither was it limited to just a small territory in the Middle East. The scripture testifies that he was to become **"heir of the world"**! And that which God started in this one nation was to spill over into other nations and was meant by God to bear global consequences of both blessing and healing.

David provides us with another witness to this national call as he prays, **"God be gracious to us and bless us, and cause His face to shine upon us—THAT Thy way may be known on the earth, Thy salvation among all nations"** (Ps 67:1-2, emphasis mine). In this priestly prayer King David expresses profound insight, far deeper than that of his generation, into the purpose of Israel's existence and blessedness. He acknowledges that God's grace and blessing are upon Israel so that all nations may know His salvation! And again David prays, **"God blesses us, THAT all the ends of the earth may fear Him"** (Ps 67:7, emphasis mine).

Israel was not created and called for her own sake nor does she belong to herself. Indeed, she was birthed, fashioned and hammered for God's own purpose from the beginning. With this **first of nations** the Lord God intensified and put into motion His redeeming plan for all humanity.

Israel's
Dilemma

The call that rested upon Israel's shoulders was as great as her inadequacy to carry it. In fact, the whole of the Old Testament account depicts the tension and the conflict between the divine call and the insufficiency of the earthen vessel.

As the newly forged nation was enroute from Egypt to the Promised Land, her very soul was to undergo a transformation. The people of Israel, at that point, were still a nation of ex-slaves! The memory of Pharaoh's whip cracking over their heads was fresh, and the cruel oppression of Egypt still overshadowed their spirits. Due to this slave mentality, many of their priorities and motives were mixed up and confused. Consequently, as the Hebrews ventured deeper into the wilderness, a major identity crisis took place. They had no clear concept of who they were before God, who God Himself was in relationship to them, or the purpose of their present trials.

As the testings intensified, their frustration increased. The wilderness on the outside continued to reveal the condition of their hearts on the inside. And while they witnessed the miraculous moving of God's hand on their behalf again and again, **"the people thirsted there for water; and they grumbled against Moses and said, 'Why, now, have you brought us up from Egypt, to kill us and our children and our livestock with thirst?' "** (Ex 17:3) Indeed, this question reflected the struggle of their hearts as the Hebrews, in effect, questioned God's intentions and trustworthiness!

Yet, despite their wrong motive, God found their frustrated and angry cry significant enough to answer, as He commanded Moses: **"Thus you shall say to the house of Jacob and tell the sons of Israel: 'You yourselves have seen what I did to the Egyptians, and how I bore you on eagles' wings, and brought you to Myself. Now then, if you will indeed obey My voice and keep My covenant, then you shall be My own possession among all the peoples, for all the earth is Mine; and you shall be to Me a kingdom of priests and a holy nation' "** (Ex 19:3-6). In effect they said, "What do you want from us, and why are we going this way?" God answered, **"You shall be to Me a kingdom of priests and a holy nation,"** thus redefining and establishing the ancient call of Abraham.

From the Lord's point of view, the world with all its depravity and decay was in need of a priest. Even as today God appoints a minister over the congregation of His people to carry out the priestly duties, so then He appointed a "priestly nation" to minister to the congregation of the nations. Israel's ministry was to bring the nations to God in **intercession** and to bring God to the nations in **demonstration!**

This was God's calling for Israel: a priestly nation, blessed and prosperous, which was to serve in holiness and righteousness. Many years later, while rebuking the backslidden northern kingdom of Israel, the Lord said through Hosea, **"I also will reject you from being My priest"** (Hos 4:6). Indeed, God has given clear recognition to the priestly role Israel was to play on behalf of the nations, and desired for her to faithfully carry it out in the global arena.

Understanding this, we can better appreciate some of the Lord's actions on earth while clothed in human flesh. We remember how the Lord Jesus called the seventy, equipping and anointing them to go out in His name. This act corresponded directly to the Sanhedrin, a body of seventy elders stationed in ancient Jerusalem. These seventy, whose origin is found in Numbers 11:16-17, were to represent the mind and the heart of God as He led His people Israel in their national call. By the time Jesus stepped onto the scene, this institution was clogged with humanistic manmade traditions, crippled by its lack of prophetic discernment, and manipulated by religious orthodoxy.

Jesus, therefore, appointed His own seventy, anointed them with His Spirit, and sent them out with fresh authority to carry out the will of God, thus fulfilling Israel's original call. Under His rule the nation now yielded divinely appointed messengers to become a blessing to others. Indeed, Israel could never carry out her mission apart from the presence of Jesus and the Spirit of the Living God. For surely, God's promise to Father Abraham to become a blessing to all nations through his seed never reached such a level of fulfillment until Jesus, the Nazarene, was born.

Isaiah captured this deep frustration in the nation's soul, this tension that stretches between her calling and her utter inability to fulfill it. While telling Israel, **"You are My Servant, Israel, in Whom I will show My glory"** (Is 49:3), God also says, **"Hear, you deaf! And look, you blind, that you may see. Who is blind but My servant, or so deaf as My messenger whom I send?"** (Is 42:18) These sobering words not only describe God's perfect servant, the Messiah; rather they speak to the nation (the earthen vessel), as well, which gave Him birth.

Truly, Israel has no other identity but to be a "servant nation," a priest for the rest of the world. And, until she embraces her call and joyfully takes upon herself the garment of a servant, even a servant to the Gentile nations, she will fail to re-enter God's graces.

Israel's dilemma is this: As long as she denies this divine purpose, she also denies herself the Divine Presence!

9

A Ransom Nation

"I am the Lord, and there is no other, the One forming light and creating darkness, causing well-being and creating calamity; I am the Lord who does all these" (Is 45:6-7).

As sons and daughters of the Living God who are increasingly led by the light of His revelation, we joyfully and wholeheartedly bow before His absolute sovereignty. The brightest of blessings and the darkest of hardships both pass through God's compassionate hands. In fact, our very failures and disappointments in life will not only work for our ultimate good in His overall purpose, but are often designed and engineered by His infinite wisdom. We need to understand, therefore, that there is a reason behind Israel's failure and a purpose behind her stumbling.

As Moses addressed the sons of Israel on the eastern plains of the River Jordan, he reiterated the words of the covenant, made further provisions and instructions for life in the land of promise, and spoke to the nation one last time: "You have seen all that the

Lord did before your eyes in the land of Egypt to Pharaoh and all
his servants and all his land; the great trials which your eyes have
seen, those great signs and wonders. Yet to this day the Lord has
not given you a heart to know, nor eyes to see, nor ears to hear"
(Deut 29:2-4).

In these words Moses gave expression to a mysterious dimension
in the working of the Lord with the nation of Israel. Here we find
that God, while leading the Israelites out of the captivity of Egypt
with signs and wonders, did not grant them a full revelation of His
purposes. The Lord of Hosts Himself led a nation out of another
nation in a traumatic and dramatic fashion. Natural disasters and
awesome displays of spiritual warfare took place, shaking the
heavens and the earth, yet God kept His people blind and deaf in
the midst of it all! Why?

Isaiah, the prophet, speaks of a similar phenomenon. As his lips
were cleansed and his life freshly anointed and commissioned for the
purposes of God in his generation, he was given these words, "Go,
and tell this people: 'Keep on listening, but do not perceive; keep on
looking, but do not understand.' Render the hearts of this people
insensitive, their ears dull, and their eyes dim, lest they see with
their eyes, hear with their ears, understand with their hearts, and
return and be healed' " (Is 6:9-10).

How can we understand such mystery? Here is God anointing
one of the greatest prophets under the old covenant, and for what
purpose? Is it not for rendering His own people deaf and blind?
What kind of God is He, that He would deliver a nation from
slavery, preserve them for millenniums, lead them by giving them
kings and priests, yet keep them in ignorance and blindness as to the
purpose of their existence? What could be His purpose in fashioning, defending and sustaining a people through centuries filled with
supernatural and miraculous events—yet keeping them from fully
understanding and embracing Him or His ways?

The Lord Jesus Himself, in Matthew 13:14, quoted Isaiah's
words, bringing their reality to bear upon His generation as well!
Indeed, Israel's tragic condition was true in Moses' days, in the days
of the prophets, and in the time when the Lord Jesus was born of
a woman. And though Israel must carry her own responsibility for
not walking with God in integrity and uprightness, yet in His

majestic sovereignty the Lord tolerated, permitted, and perhaps even engineered their blindness, deafness and calloused hearts. All this, in the words of the prophet, **"lest they see . . . hear . . . understand . . . and return and be healed."**

Even the sound of these words is almost inconceivable! Could it be that God Himself would deny His own people the conviction and the grace by which they could repent and be healed? And, what could be the purpose behind such a plan?

As numerous as the possible answers to this question could be, God's Word gives us only one clear answer, as Paul declares concerning ancient Israel that, **"by their transgression salvation has come to the Gentiles"** (Rom 11:11). Indeed, the apostle observes Israel's rejection from God's point of view, as he links their tragedy directly to the greatest blessing the heathen nations of the world could ever receive—reconciliation to God through the mediation of the Messiah!

Furthermore, the apostle adds that **"from the standpoint of the gospel they [the Jews] are enemies for your [the nations'] sake"** (Rom 11:28). Thus, in God's wisdom and reason, He not only allowed one nation to become an enemy of the gospel **for the sake** of others, but in the final analysis this was His best way to accomplish His plan of redemption for the world.

Truly, apart from the inspiration and help of the Holy Spirit, we could never understand such a mystery. Ethnic Israel became, in the sovereignty of God, a **ransom nation**—a people who would be rejected almost sacrificially on behalf of others, and for their sake. And, while only the Lord Jesus could serve in the office of the Sacrificial Lamb of God, atoning for the sin of the world, still the scriptures clearly testify to that principle of a **ransom nation**, whereby one people is given for the sake of another.

The prophet Isaiah gives expression to these severe and trying dynamics of God's righteousness and sovereignty, as the Lord comforts Israel with these words: **"For I am the Lord your God, the Holy One of Israel, your Savior; I have given Egypt as your RANSOM, Cush and Seba in your place. Since you are precious in My sight, since you are honored and I love you, I will give other men in your place and other peoples in EXCHANGE for your life"** (Is 43:3-4, emphasis mine). Furthermore, we find the same principle not only in the arena of nations but also on a personal level, as scripture teaches us that, **"The wicked is a ransom for the righteous, and the treacherous is in the place of the upright"** (Prov 21:18).

Obviously, there is room in the righteous dealings of the Lord for one to be denied so that another can be accepted. We must learn from Paul's words, **"Now I rejoice in my sufferings for your sake, and in my flesh I do my share on behalf of His body (which is the church) in filling up that which is lacking in Christ's afflictions"** (Col 1:24).

Surely, the apostle knew perfectly well that Christ's sufferings and atonement were sufficient for the redemption of the world; surely, he believed that this supreme sacrifice could never be improved upon or repeated. And yet, he also knew the necessity of the sharing of the sufferings of Christ—the truth that every Christian generation is granted the privilege and honor of carrying a portion of the very sufferings and dying of the Son of God, thus standing as ambassadors of Christ for the world around them.

In light of this, we can better understand and come to appreciate the divine drama of appointing one entire nation to be given for the sake of others. Not only was Israel at enmity with God **for the sake** of other nations (Rom 11:28), but the apostolic declaration to these nations is that they **"have been shown mercy because of their [Israel's] disobedience"** (Rom 11:30). Indeed, for God's mercies which are in Christ to fall upon the heathen nations of the world, first Israel had to deny and disown the Messiah, thus releasing Him to the nations.

Israel, who was called to be a priest unto God, serving the nations of the world in intercession and demonstration, might have reached her highest pinnacle of service in losing her national vitality and life on behalf of the heathen. Such was necessary so that the seed of heaven, born of her, could be sown, take root, and blossom in the soil of the nations!

10

Israel—God's Object Lesson

The historic saga of Israel demonstrates that, while yet in spiritual blindness and moral nakedness, God still speaks through her. As we look deeply and prayerfully into the genetic code of that "first of nations" and into the uniqueness of that "ransom nation," we discover principal truths pertaining to the very nature and ways of God. In the life and history of the Jewish people, God's election, sovereignty, judgment, great ability, and bountiful mercies were first revealed. The Holy Spirit is our teacher, and Israel is the blackboard upon which He draws His illustrations.

God's Election

In telling the story of the coming forth of the chosen nation, Paul clarifies her origin. He explains in Romans, chapter 9, that although Father Abraham had more than one son, it would be **"through Isaac [that] your descendants will be named"** (Rom 9:7).

The Lord obviously elected a specific lineage through which to accomplish His purpose, even to the point of choosing one brother over another.

As this divine plan unfolds, the apostle speaks of Rebekah's twins. Here are two sons who were not only of the same parents (unlike the brothers Ishmael and Isaac who were born to different mothers) but were actual twins, closely and intimately related. And yet, the scripture says concerning them that, **"though the twins were not yet born, and had not done anything good or bad, in order that God's purpose according to His choice might stand, not because of works, but because of Him who calls, it was said to her, 'The older will serve the younger.' Just as it is written, 'Jacob I loved, but Esau I hated' "** (Rom 9:11-13).

Indeed, these are difficult words. They challenge every humanistic philosophy and every self-centered aspiration. God places His Word as a mirror of truth before the face of humanity and declares, **"I will have mercy on whom I have mercy, and I will have compassion on whom I have compassion"** (Rom 9:15).

Through the election of Israel, undeserving and unworthy as she may be, a humbling and grace-filled truth comes to the church. It is God who chose us, God who pursued us, God who wooed, convicted and pleaded with us so that we might believe, repent and be saved. It is God who initiates everything and continues to put within us the Spirit and the unction to pursue Him.

The question, "When did you find the Lord?" is symptomatic of a church defiled with humanistic thinking! The true question should be, "When did the Lord find you, and in what condition were you when He first gave you grace to believe?" He is the one who elects us by His own choice, and Israel is the backdrop, the prototype, and the ongoing historical proof of God's election!

God's Sovereignty

Not only do we find unmistakable and undeniable evidence for God's election embedded deep within the people of Israel, but we find that there is more. The apostle, in writing about the Jewish nation, proclaimed that they **"are Israelites, to whom belongs the adoption as sons and the glory and the covenants and the giving of the Law and the temple service and the promises, whose are the** fathers, and from whom is the Christ according to the flesh, who is over all, God blessed forever. Amen" (Rom 9:4-5). Here, the apostle makes an emphatic declaration that the sonship, the glory, the covenants (old and new), the worship, and the promises still "belong" to Israel. Indeed, this one nation became the recipient of much undeserved divine favor and privilege.

The humanistic mind would rise up and protest: How can this be? How can God choose one over the other? How dare He prefer one twin, one brother, one family or nation above another? It is not fair! It is not right! And, the root question is: "Who is God anyway to so determine and rule over our lives?"

That same question echoes all the way back to the Garden of Eden. It was that questioning of God's sovereignty and right to determine our affairs that gave rise to the original disobedience. Down the blood line this question flowed through Adam's descendants, reaching to the builders of the Tower of Babel and to the leaders and shapers of nations. They still cry: "Who is this God? Must we obey His will?" And, as the psalmist records, **"The kings of the earth take their stand, and the rulers take counsel together against the Lord and against His Anointed: 'Let us tear their fetters apart, and cast away their cords from us!' "** (Ps 2:2-3)

The scripture answers that humanistic battle cry, **"Who are you, O man, who answers back to God? The thing molded will not say to the molder, 'Why did you make me like this,' will it? Or does not the potter have a right over the clay, to make from the same lump one vessel for honorable use, and another for common use?"** (Rom 9:20-21)

Indeed, in Israel's saga, God confronts man's disobedience and lust for independence by demonstrating His sovereign authority over the affairs of men and nations! It is through the raising of that one nation, and His exclusive dealings with her, that God proves His right and authority to perform His will and His pleasure in the earth!

God is not subject to His creation nor to the opinions of His creatures. He declares that He is **"the One forming light and creating darkness, causing well-being and creating calamity; I am the Lord who does all these . . . Woe to the one who quarrels with his Maker"** (Is 45:7-9). And though God's patience can stretch for a very long time, the consequences of man's unrepented assertion of self will surely come.

Indeed, until this very day, that ancient lesson continues to challenge the nations and the powers of this world. Humanly speaking, Israel should have ceased from existence long ago. Politically, economically, and geographically the Jewish nation was "dead" for millenniums, buried in the soil of other nations. And yet, it is now resurrected! In our century alone, the world witnessed the supernatural regathering of Israel from the four corners of the earth and the amazing reclamation and restoration of the land of promise. God is aggressively announcing His sovereignty to the powers of this world!

Emperors, kings, dictators, politicians, pseudo-Christians, and spiritual powers and principalities have sought to nullify this sovereignty of God. They have all failed to successfully resist His will, and will continue to fail until the last rebellion is crushed! Israel, the very proof of God's final authority and absolute dominion, still stands and will continue to stand.

God's Judgments

Coupled with God's sovereign rule over His creation is His moral duty and responsibility to judge. As Abraham cried out, **"Shall not the Judge of all the earth deal justly?"** (Gen 18:25) The Lord God, by the very virtue of perfection, holiness and sovereignty, **must judge** right from wrong. For the wicked, His judgments are their retribution; for the righteous, His judgments are His mercies. **"For when the earth experiences Thy judgments the inhabitants of the world learn righteousness"** (Is 26:9).

We find the ungodly resisting and cringing beneath the righteous judgments of God. Their fists shaking heavenward, their mouths filled with blasphemies, these slaves of unrighteousness are unable to perceive God's judgments as His mercies. To them, and to the church, Israel continues to testify!

Paul, after speaking in very clear terms of God's election and sovereignty as portrayed in the saga of Israel, is not at all embarrassed to also use the Jewish nation as an object lesson pertaining to the judgments of God. Indeed, to the degree of the privilege and benefits of being chosen and called by God, the recipients of such graces are also held accountable.

Israel, in the sovereignty of God, failed to heed all His commandments. The nation did not believe, trust or obey His words. Thus, in His judgment of that nation God is teaching all humanity a most sobering lesson. The scripture testifies, **"They did not all heed the glad tidings; for Isaiah says, 'Lord, who has believed our report?' "** (Rom 10:16) And as the apostle then describes God's gracious invitation through the Messiah toward all nations, he adds, **"as for Israel He says, 'All the day long I have stretched out My hands to a disobedient and obstinate people' "** (Rom 10:21).

God does not hide the truth. And even as He greatly raised and elevated Israel, so now He greatly chastises her: **"Just as it is written, 'God gave them a spirit of stupor, eyes to see not and ears to hear not, down to this very day' "** (Rom 11:8). And indeed, is this not the veil prophesied of old that is still covering the eyes, the hearts, and the understanding of most of Israel? Is this not the **"partial hardening"** Paul spoke of in Romans 11:25? What greater judgment is there than to be violently hurled from land to land through centuries of suffering and persecution, miraculously preserved, yet never knowing why?

Moses prophesied, seeing the future calamity, **"Because you did not serve the Lord your God with joy and a glad heart . . . you shall serve your enemies . . . the Lord will bring a nation against you from afar . . . Moreover, the Lord will scatter you among all peoples, from one end of the earth to the other . . . among those nations you shall find no rest . . . there the Lord will give you a trembling heart . . . your life shall hang in doubt . . . In the morning you shall say, 'Would that it were evening!' And at evening you shall say, 'Would that it were morning!' "** (Deut 28:47-49, 64-67)

Indeed, here lies the historical judgment of Israel—the most traumatic and painful saga of a nation stumbling from one century to the next, driven from land to land with no rest nor comfort for her soul. Truly, as it has been said, "God's wheels may grind slow, but they grind exceedingly fine."

Were these judgments justified? Could God really require complete obedience and faith? Was He right in blinding a people, then punishing them for their blindness? Can God do such things and remain true to His nature? These, and more, are the questions that plague the carnal mind. And yet, the reality of both scriptural prophecy and Israel's history confronts the motives of our hearts as we behold God's chosen nation, His first-born, under the unrelenting rod of His righteous judgment! Both the world and the church must heed this lesson.

For those who believe, there is the ultimate comfort of Abraham's assurance, "**Shall not the Judge of all the earth deal justly?**" (Gen 18:25) And as Hosea cried, "**Come, let us return to the Lord. For He has torn us, but He will heal us; He has wounded us, but He will bandage us. He will revive us after two days; He will raise us up on the third day that we may live before Him**" (Hos 6:1-2). Indeed, in the Lord's righteous dealings, even the most severe judgments are redemptive in nature and for the purpose of producing a more glorious fruit.

Again Moses, seeing the end of God's judgments upon Israel, prophesied: "**So it shall be when all of these things have come upon you, the blessing and the curse which I have set before you, and you call them to mind in all nations where the Lord your God has banished you ... then the Lord your God will restore you from captivity ... will circumcise your heart ... will inflict all these curses on your enemies and on those who hate you ... will prosper you abundantly ... if you obey the Lord your God ... if you turn to the Lord your God with all your heart and soul**" (Deut 30:1-10). Indeed, in God's judgments are His mercies. They purge, test and perfect all who humble themselves and submit to His dealings without resisting or questioning His authority.

God is our judge, not only in the final judgment but also today. His judgments are righteous, and they will produce in us the desired fruit of godly character and holiness. Surely He has the right and the duty to judge, and in Israel's history He teaches us this vital truth.

The only proper and wise response to God's judgments and discipline is, indeed, found in the words of Eliphaz to Job: "**Behold, how happy is the man whom God reproves, so do not despise the discipline of the Almighty. For He inflicts pain, and gives relief; He wounds, and His hands also heal**" (Job 5:17-18).

God is Able

As the progressive dealings of God with the Jewish people unfold under Paul's pen, he arrives at a most comforting and encouraging lesson. Having spoken of the severity of God's judgments which go hand in hand with His election, the apostle unveils the reason for and the outcome of these sufferings. Romans, chapter 11, declares that Israel's judgment will be followed by glory. A healing so great and a grace so rich are to come upon that one nation that the whole world will be affected by her restoration.

But how could that be? How can a people so scattered, a land so devastated, and a national soul so bruised for so long ever be restored? Can the course of events really be reversed after thousands of years? Can ancient prophecies and promises really come to life and fulfillment before the eyes of a bewildered world? As Isaiah cried, **"Who has heard such a thing? Who has seen such things? Can a land be born in one day? Can a nation be brought forth all at once?"** (Is 66:8) And to Ezekiel God said, **"Son of man, can these bones live?"** (Ez 37:3)

The apostle answers these questions as he writes to the Roman disciples concerning this supernatural and promised restoration of the Jewish nation, saying, **"they also, if they do not continue in their unbelief, WILL be grafted in; for GOD IS ABLE to graft them in again"** (Rom 11:23, emphasis mine). Could it be that the answer to these crucial questions concerning Israel's destiny is in these few words, **"God is able"**? Can this compact and brief declaration really change the course of human history? Indeed, what a simple and profound answer to man's dilemma!

Could there be any more reassuring words in all of the languages of man? Could there be any doubt, any fear or hesitation in our hearts in light of such a promise? **Our God is able!** He is able to perform all that He has promised! He is able to restore all that is lost! He is able to heal all that is broken, to straighten all that is crooked, and to make right all that is wrong! **Our God is able!**

If He, indeed, is able to restore and graft the Jew back in, will He find it too difficult to restore all who call upon His name? If He is able to erase centuries of national pain and blindness in one swift wind of revelation, will He find it too difficult to perfect His victory in our small personal battles?

Again, Israel is an object lesson—this time a lesson of faith, of hope, and of trust in our God. Is there anything in our lives He does not know? Any chamber of our hearts He cannot reach? Anyone He cannot restore, or any nation He cannot heal?

It was Jesus Himself who taught us that **"all things are possible with God"** (Mark 10:27). And again, **"All things are possible to him who believes"** (Mark 9:23). We must build up our faith, hold onto His promises, and wait on Him with trusting hearts, for our **"God is able."**

God's Mercies

The best part in the unfolding of God's object lessons through the nation of Israel is yet to come. As the apostle continues to pour out by revelation the wealth and the riches of God's purposes in and through the Jewish people, he brings it all to its glorious conclusion.

Not only has he shown that Israel's enmity with the gospel is for the sake of the ungodly nations (Rom 11:28), and not only does he declare with great assurance that the Jewish people are still beloved and called of God (Rom 11:28-29), but he points to the reason behind these dramatic events.

Paul writes to the Gentile disciples, **"For just as you once were disobedient to God, but now have been shown mercy because of their [the Jews] disobedience,"** God wills that, **"because of the mercy shown to you [Gentiles] they [the Jews] also may now be shown mercy"** (Rom 11:30-31). Indeed, the deepest motive in the very heart and plan of God is to reveal and exercise His mercies!

In other words, the heathen and the disobedient nations of the world became the recipients of the mercies of God through Christ **because** of Israel's disobedience and rejection of Him! And now, as the divine plan continues to unfold, it is **because** of the mercy shown to the nations that Israel, too, will receive mercy. Indeed, God's ways are not as the ways of man!

It is not beyond our God to create all things, to shape nations, cultures and societies, and to bring forth the wonder of Israel and the glory of the church in order to fully manifest and display His great mercies. Thus the apostle concludes, **"God has shut up all in disobedience THAT He might show mercy to all"** (Rom 11:32, emphasis mine).

The final chapter of God's dealings with the Jewish people is all about mercy. The regathering to the land, the establishment of the modern state of Israel, the miraculous protection through the continuous wars, and the present Jewish exodus out of Russia and other lands all tell of His mercies. This is the last and final lesson the world and the church will learn from Israel. As the mercies of God are rekindled over these undeserving people and their devastated land, bringing healing, restoration and revival, we see, indeed, the concluding chapter of our age!

When Moses asked to see the glory of the Lord (Ex 33:18), God brought him up onto the mountain and then descended in the cloud. **"Then the Lord passed by . . . and proclaimed, 'The Lord, the Lord God, compassionate and gracious, slow to anger, and abounding in lovingkindness and truth; who keeps lovingkindness for thousands, who forgives iniquity, transgression and sin"** (Ex 34:6-7). In answer to Moses' request to see God's glory, the Lord showed him His compassion, graciousness, and lovingkindness. Surely, this is the revelation of the glory of God!

There is no higher or greater insight into the nature and the essence of our God. There is no better lesson we can learn from Israel than this: **"It is of the Lord's mercies that we are not consumed, because His compassions fail not"** (Lam 3:22 KJV). Indeed, with Israel God demonstrates to the fullest His nature and His ways. Such rich and awesome expression of the Creator's heart is found in no other nation. The rest of humanity stands without excuse before such a timeless display of God's sovereignty, severity and mercy.

11

Who is a Jew?

"Thus says the Lord, Who gives the sun for light by day, and the fixed order of the moon and the stars for light by night, Who stirs up the sea so that its waves roar; the Lord of hosts is His name: 'If this fixed order departs from before Me,' declares the Lord, 'Then the offspring of Israel also shall cease from being a nation before Me forever' " (Jer 31:35-36).

It is essential in the economy of God for the people of Israel to maintain their unique identity as a nation before Him! While other nations formed and later collapsed, having the identity of the masses changed and transformed time and time again, the essence of Israel's identity was miraculously preserved. In fact, God's Word strongly emphasizes that the Jews will never cease from being a nation before Him! Thus, we understand that, though the nation underwent deep and traumatic changes during and after the Babylonian exile, the essence of their identity was never to be diminished or even questioned, but rather discovered and rediscovered in each successive generation.

As we pursue this subject, we must remember that no single writing can offer a satisfying answer or do justice to this question. Over the millenniums of Jewish existence, entire movements have paraded the theme of Jewish identity; national figures rose and fell over this issue, and the governments of the modern state of Israel continuously grapple with the weight of that question to this day!

The fact is that so much has been invested into the identity of the Jewish people. By now, it is an amazing collage of divine purposes, ethnic flavors, biblical moral codes, ancient cultural treasures, and a recorded national history that goes back further than any other modern nation. Jewish identity is presently a spiritual, national and geographic mystery, the key to which is in the hand of our Creator alone.

The Patriarchs are the Root

" 'Listen to me, you who pursue righteousness, who seek the Lord: Look to the rock from which you were hewn, and to the quarry from which you were dug. Look to Abraham your father, and to Sarah who gave birth to you in pain; when he was one I called him, then I blessed him and multiplied him.' Indeed the Lord will comfort Zion; He will comfort all her waste places. And her wilderness He will make like Eden" (Is 51:1-3).

As God speaks of the restoration of Israel, He is calling the nation, while yet entangled in bondage and affliction, to re-establish her true identity by looking to the man who fathered her. For if to be a Jew one is to be properly linked to this historic root of the national life and heritage, then one must discover the identity of Father Abraham!

Was Abraham a Jew? By no means! In the traditional and rabbinical sense of Judaism, Abraham was not born a Jew nor did he ever become one through some manmade ceremony. The man Abraham was born in the land of the Chaldeans (modern day Iraq), 500 miles away from the territory that, 500 years later, would be called Judea. The only ethnic identification the scriptures give Father Abraham is that he was a **Hebrew** (Gen 14:13), a title undoubtedly derived from his ancestor Eber, Shem's great-grandson, who preceded Abraham by seven generations (Gen 11:10-27). This title simply denotes in the Hebrew language "someone who crossed over from the other side; a sojourner, a pioneer."

And indeed, it was the Lord God who said to Abraham, **"Go forth from your country, and from your relatives and from your father's house, to the land which I will show you"** (Gen 12:1). Abraham's obedience and devotion to God's will provide the main ingredients which characterize the father of the nation of Israel and define his identity.

The man, Abram, became "Abraham" when God's involvement in his life increased to the point that the promises were sealed in covenant. Indeed, God was not only incorporating His purposes but also His own divine self into the life of this man and his descendants. Father Abraham still stands as that rock from which Israel was hewn, that person who has forsaken his earthly roots while finding new identity in the heavenly call!

Abraham's life, which speaks of courage, faith and obedience, brought forth Isaac, whose life speaks of faithfulness and submission to his father. He, in turn, brought forth Jacob, a life which denotes renewal and regeneration, and whose name God later changed to **Israel**. It was at the end of Jacob's night-long struggle with the Lord on the way back to the Promised Land that he acknowledged and confessed his flesh nature. At that point of repentance and humility, God gave him a new name and a new identity—**Israel**—one who has authority, position, and standing with God!

Examining the unfolding of Israel's history, we find how the Lord Himself firmly established these two titles, **Hebrew** and **Israelite**, as the very essence and distinctiveness of the national character. It was in these titles, born of both the obedience and the repentance of the patriarchs, that the emerging nation would find perpetual identity and strength, as well as a sense of purpose and destiny.

In addition to the patriarchs, we find in the life of Paul, who was a zealous Jewish rabbi wholly given in the service of the Messiah, an excellent example of a Jewish disciple speaking of his own identity. As he related his personal biography to the Philippian disciples, while tearing down the stronghold of Jewish legalistic pride (Phil 3:2-7), he identified himself nationally as an **Israelite** and ethnically as a **Hebrew** (verse 5), and does not use the term **Jewish** at all.

Again, when Paul bared his heart to the Corinthian church while defending his apostleship, he proclaimed his earthly identity to be **Hebrew, Israelite,** and a descendant of Abraham (2 Cor 11:22). Here, too, he did not find it necessary to call himself Jewish.

Yet, we fully understand and acknowledge that Paul was Jewish, as he himself mentions elsewhere, as he was born of Jewish descent, was circumcised on the eighth day, celebrated the biblical feasts, and kept the traditions of the fathers. However, submitting to the authority of the scriptures, we must agree that Paul's earthly identity went deeper than the term "Jewish" implies, and reached into the "Hebrew" and "Israelite" roots. Thus the question surfaces: What is the difference?

Shaken Foundations

Throughout history, from the time of the patriarchs, the nation of Israel kept evolving, changing and developing. Their captivity in Egypt, the exodus, the wilderness, and the conquest of the Promised Land became historical facts as centuries passed. And while God's nation was uniquely called by the name of **Israel** throughout its early years (as recorded from Genesis to Kings), a change was introduced during the reign of Rehoboam, Solomon's proud and rebellious son (1 Kings 12:6-20).

As prophesied, the nation was torn in two under his unrighteous rule, as the northern kingdom broke away. Rehoboam was left with two tribes only, and a new kingdom was now established—the **Judean Kingdom**—a separate political, social and spiritual entity. And, though this Judean kingdom was the house of the beloved David, it was born in rebellion, foolishness and shame!

In time, the northern kingdom of **Israel** was swallowed up, as Assyria swept it into exile, and the surviving southern kingdom of **Judah** now carried on the national identity. We must remember that this new national identity, **Judah,** was not divinely given and carried only limited tribal and territorial authority, as it was the sad product of Rehoboam's pride and presumption.

The name **"Jew"** (derived from Judah, meaning "God's praiser" in the Hebrew), which had its origin in the Judean southern kingdom, came into full acceptance during yet a darker hour of that kingdom. It was as Judah was carried away into the Babylonian captivity, entering a season of divine judgment and national shame, that the name, **Jew** or "Yehoodi" in the Hebrew language, was permanently fastened to the exiled Hebrew remnant. And by whom? Not by God nor by any of His prophets, but rather by the unbelieving and ungodly heathen in whose midst Israel was now dwelling.

For the very first time in its history, that **Hebrew** nation, that family of **Israelites**, is identified nationally as **Jews** by its oppressors. And, indeed, we often find in the exilic and post-exilic writings, such as Esther and Nehemiah, the name **Jews** or "Yehoodim," which rarely appeared earlier. Sadly, this name, which was conceived in rebellion and pride under Rehoboam's rule, was now fully adopted under conditions of exile, captivity and national shame.

A major shift took place, and an almost irreversible change occurred within the nation's identity. Now, emerging from its captivity as a humbled remnant, the survivors are no longer known as **Hebrews**—not even as **Israelites**; now they are the **"Jews,"** a different name implying a changed national identity!

From this point on, we recognize a subtle drifting away from the authentic and original biblical roots. New ideological foundations crept in, as the "Babylonian Talmud," compiled by Jewish sages while in exile, became, in time, a substitute for divine guidance. Volumes upon volumes of traditions, regulations, and teachings of man were added over the centuries, as the prophetic voice faded away!

Divinely appointed kings to lead the nation rose no more; they now were replaced by governors and administrators, most of them foreign. And, apart from a few years of sweet and blood-bought freedom, the nation was, from here on, ruled by strangers, held captive, longing for the liberty that only God can give. Indeed, Israel became very "Jewish" as her posture toward God, her religious philosophy, and even her very identity underwent great changes. She now clothed herself with garments of shame, remorse and sorrow as she was carried off again to sojourn among the heathen nations at the beginning of our era!

Moses prophesied, while looking into the distant future of the national life, that **"the Lord will scatter you among all peoples, from one end of the earth to the other . . . among those nations you shall find no rest . . . there the Lord will give you a trembling heart . . . In the morning you shall say, 'Would that it were evening!' And at** evening you shall say, 'Would that it were morning!' " (Deut 28:64-67) Indeed, these difficult words were fulfilled in the most devastating fashion as the nation of Israel was violently swept into two thousand years of struggling through the valley of the shadow of death. So great was the shaking and the loss that it would take nothing short of a miracle to bring restoration.

We would be safe to say that no other nation or people group on earth was required to endure what Israel endured. The national life was so devastated, scattered and shattered that it was certainly beyond human means and power to heal. Yet, God committed Himself to their restoration.

Indeed, not only does God Himself confirm Israel's perpetual existence as a people, but His Word strongly emphasizes that they will never cease from being a **nation** before Him! Thus, we understand that, though the nation was undergoing deep and traumatic changes during and after the Babylonian exile, the essence of her existence was never to be questioned. In other words, it is essential for the people of Israel to maintain their unique identity as a nation before God in order to fulfill the scripture.

New Beginnings

Emerging from two millenniums of exile and shame, we find the soul of the Jewish nation, which was laden with suffering, anxiety and rejection, now bringing with it a fresh breath. That which was lost, robbed, and watered down in the dusty pages of history is being resurrected with power in our century.

The ancient national soul and identity, which was emasculated through sin, unbelief, and perpetual persecutions, now re-surfaced in the hearts of those who returned from the captivity. Indeed, **"When the Lord brought back the captive ones of Zion, we were like those who dream. Then our mouth was filled with laughter, and our tongue with joyful shouting"** (Ps 126:1-2). The very fabric of the Jewish people has been regaining ancient strength and valor as they have returned to the land, defending in warfare their inheritance and rebuilding ancient ruins.

For surely, a new window opened up in the Jewish national soul as the early pioneers reclaimed and resettled the ancient homeland in the last one hundred years. The Jews, who while in exile had to drink deep from the cup of tradition to maintain their distinct identity, were now sinking their fingers deep into the soil of the land itself, reconnecting to and drawing from the authentic historical and geographic roots.

Indeed, there is a promise in God's Word. Indeed, there is an unsettled issue in the Father's heart. There is a loud proclamation from the heavenlies that these cut-off natural branches shall re-enter the blessed olive tree.

But, how shall they re-enter: as exiled, oppressed unprophetic, religious-minded, and unspiritual people? Impossible! Rather, the scripture promises that they will be grafted back in and be restored to God's calling and purposes as they excavate the ancient, true and God-given identity from the depth of the national soul—that **Hebrew and Israelite** essence!

There is a treasure buried deep within Israel's corporate consciousness. It is a long-lost treasure—a rare commodity that God Himself invested in the heart of this people. This treasure must be rediscovered and brought into full light as an end-time offering of an end-time generation. It is not the precious Jewish traditions, the high morals, or the puffed up and prideful facade so often cherished by this people. No! The real treasure is yet deeper within.

There is a people on earth for whom the Bible is their own history, and not merely spiritual allegories; there is a nation who tasted real freedom as they crossed the Red Sea, who knew the flavor of the original manna in the wilderness, and who let out a loud shout and saw Jericho's walls collapse before them in a heap of rubble. There is a people who fought the actual Philistines, who slew real giants, who claimed and possessed a tangible land, and who beheld the glory cloud come down upon and fill the temple of their God. **There is a nation on earth today which carries deep within its blood and bosom a purpose and a call which must be rediscovered, cultivated and perfected yet one last time!**

What will it be like when such a people come alive unto God? What hidden treasure will then explode within the church, the very body and bride of our Lord Jesus, as these ancient brethren are quickened again and revived into their true identity, **Hebrew** and **Israelite**, a warring and a worshipping nation? Indeed, that **one new man** company, which shall see the fulfillment of the age and shall satisfy the Father's heart in that hour, is beyond our current comprehension. And yet we hold the vision; we travail for this hour to come upon the earth, praying that the ancient Hebrew ingredient will be restored into the body of Messiah.

Therefore, we Jews must repent of all prideful self-sufficiency and give up all unnecessary cargo (as did Paul) in order to find our God-given identity. The Gentile, on the other hand, must repent of all prideful insecurities, and pray that Israel may rise out of her ignorance and blindness and into her true identity before God.

The Jewish nation is to emerge again as a Hebrew and an Israelite nation: **Hebrews**—those crossing over from the other side, as did Abraham, making the transition with faith, courage and obedience. And **Israelites**—those admitting to the carnal nature, as did Jacob, in order to receive a new nature and a new identity, one of authority and standing before God. **Indeed, the true Jew is characterized by the obedience of faith and the humility of repentance!**

The church of the Lord Jesus will soon understand the importance of her intercession for Israel. The hand of God, through the intercession of His servants, will turn the key to unlock that ancient cellar where the real treasures, the identity, and the calling have been gathering dust for so long. And open that treasure they shall, in intercession and travail, in shouts of victory and tears of compassion, so that the light of God may shine in and reveal who the nation of Israel really is before Him.

SECTION THREE:

The Promise to Restore

Introduction

" 'And it will come about that as I have watched over them to pluck up, to break down, to overthrow, to destroy, and to bring disaster, so I will watch over them to build and to plant,' declares the Lord" (Jer 31:28).

Ironically, while much of the church recognizes that the background, scriptures, covenants, and promises came to us through Israel, which is the foundational community of God's one olive tree, most continue to ignore the fact that God still has a purpose for this people to fulfill. This ignorance, blinding us from perceiving and participating in God's end-time purposes, is not only detrimental to the well-being of the church, but is often induced and inflamed by demonic forces, fueled with deception and hostility.

For millenniums, the Deceiver has done his utmost to blur the church's vision, confuse her thoughts, and harden her heart to the truth of who Israel is in God's plan. Ceaselessly, Satan assaults this revelation, attempting to replace it with deceitful misconceptions. The enemy always sows poisonous tares in God's good field.

The Word of the Lord, however, is from **everlasting to everlasting** and God is **"watching over** [His] **Word to perform it"** (Jer 1:12). Thus, in a supernatural fashion, ancient prophecies find their long-awaited fulfillment in our day.

12

Dynamics
of Restoration

The Apostle's Heart

As we approach the Word of God, we must search not only for the obvious doctrinal substance, but also for the life and spirit of the Word as it was given to us through the inspired vessel.

With this in mind, let us consider the depth of the apostle's cry: "I am telling the truth in Christ, I am not lying, my conscience bearing me witness in the Holy Spirit, that I have great sorrow and unceasing grief in my heart. For I could wish that I myself were accursed, separated from Christ for the sake of my brethren, my kinsmen according to the flesh, who are Israelites" (Rom 9:1-4).

Paul actually wished that he was lost, cut off from the Savior, and damned in hell for the sake of his brethren, the Israelites! He is ready to assign himself to everlasting destruction, forfeiting God's great gift of salvation, on behalf of his kinsmen! Can we even begin to appreciate the depth of anguish and the breadth of revelation residing in Paul's spirit, driving him to such an extreme expression?

Paul was not a man to speak lightly of weighty matters, or one to be manipulated by emotional reactions. He is the one who boldly proclaimed, "[God] **was pleased to reveal His Son in me**" (Gal 1:15-16), and we certainly know that Paul had no other purpose for his life on earth but to know and serve the risen Son of God. His devastating statement was born neither of superficial sentiment for his lost kindred or soulish grief alone. Rather, something profound and awesome must have driven him to such depth of agony and anguish of spirit. In this personal "Gethsemane," the apostle wanted to perish and have his name blotted out of the Book of Life for the sake of his Jewish brethren!

What was it that so stirred the heart of this man? What knowledge did he possess concerning Israel's restoration to God that we have not yet perceived? What was the great significance of the salvation of Israel that was so important to the apostle's heart that he would sacrifice himself for it? Could it be that the nation's restoration, envisioned by the prophets of old and proclaimed by the apostle himself, holds great value far beyond the individual salvation of so many souls? Could it be that the ramifications of Israel's deliverance from sin and unbelief will reverberate throughout the whole earth with unprecedented blessings? Is it possible that Israel's healing will serve as the harbinger for the healing of all nations?

The Nature of the Restoration

As the Lord looks upon the nations of the world and upon Israel, He asks, "**Have you not observed what this people have spoken, saying, 'The two families [Judah and Israel] which the Lord chose, He has rejected them'? Thus they despise My people, no longer are they as a nation in their sight**" (Jer 33:24). Tragically, these words depict the confession and position of many. While they recognize that the nation of Israel had something to do with the beginnings of God's redeeming activity in the past, they often deny her a future role and purpose. The world increasingly attempts to deny Israel's place, even as it manifests so clearly in international politics. And sadly, much of the church still fails to comprehend God's plan, thus also ignoring Israel's place!

The fact is that this same prophecy of Jeremiah continues in declaring the Lord's promise to restore: **"If My covenant for day and night stand not, and the fixed patterns of heaven and earth I have not established, then I would reject the descendants of Jacob and David My servant, not taking from his descendants rulers over the descendants of Abraham, Isaac, and Jacob. But I WILL restore their fortunes and WILL have mercy on them"** (Jer 33:25-26, emphasis mine).

While many believe that all God has for the Jews is to be individually saved and brought as scattered sheep into the sheep pen, still the scripture gives us ample evidence that God has reserved a **national restoration** for Israel. Jeremiah rebuked the nations who reject and despise Israel by claiming the Jews are **"no longer . . . a nation."**

Rather, in God's defense of His own purpose and counsel, He proclaims that Israel will re-emerge and re-enter His graces as a **nation!**

The prophet Zechariah adds this testimony regarding Israel's national salvation: **"And I will pour out on the house of David and on the inhabitants of Jerusalem, the Spirit of grace and of supplication . . . and the land will mourn . . . all the families that remain . . . In that day a fountain will be opened for the house of David and for the inhabitants of Jerusalem, for sin and for impurity"** (Zech 12:10-13:1). The prophetic picture given here is that of a whole nation and a whole land baptized in conviction, repentance and healing!

Amazing as it is, Israel is the only nation concerning which the scriptures promise a national repentance and healing. Indeed, a great harvest is being gathered from every nation and tribe under the sun, yet these are but remnants from their nations, while Israel still awaits the fulfillment of the promised national revival.

This testimony is repeatedly expressed through Isaiah, Ezekiel, Jeremiah, Hosea, and other prophetic voices. All spoke directly and with great anticipation of this future healing of the nation. After the decreed judgments and chastisement are fulfilled, God's Word always points toward the promised restoration. For otherwise, how are we to grasp the full scope and magnitude resounding in Isaiah's words, " 'Comfort, O comfort My people,' says your God. 'Speak kindly to Jerusalem; and call out to her, that her warfare has ended, that her iniquity has been removed, that she has received of the Lord's hand double for all her sins' " (Is 40:1-2).

There is a day coming, and is already upon us, when God's last days promises for Israel are undeniably surfacing and finding fulfillment. History itself bears witness to this national restoration that is presently unfolding before the eyes of a confused and unbelieving world, as God continues to draw the scattered Jewish communities into the national homeland. And surely, this resurrection in the natural dimension will continue on until the spiritual dimension is also restored, for what God has purposed for this nation, He will fulfill!

The Purpose of the Restoration

The sovereignty of God determines the affairs of man, and He alone decrees the falling and rising of nations. Historically, Israel was called, equipped and blessed to carry out her mission, and yet she failed. The righteous judgments of the Lord fell upon her, and the nation passed through the valley of the shadow of death for centuries upon centuries. Still the prophetic Word stands firm, defying the counsel and frailty of men and defining the outcome of history. In spite of natural and supernatural resistance, and despite Israel's own sin and unbelief, the unchangeable decree of the Lord of heaven and earth is for her to return to Him and be healed!

Paul gave ample expression to this truth while addressing the Roman disciples. This epistle is the most systematic and comprehensive theological presentation in New Testament writings. And right in the context of revealing man's depravity, God's righteousness, the plan of salvation, and the nature of spiritual life—the Holy Spirit penned the revelation of Israel by committing three chapters to her calling, rejection and restoration!

Concerning Israel Paul wrote, "they did not stumble so as to fall, did they? May it never be!" (Rom 11:11) The apostle makes a clear distinction here as he assures the readers that while this nation, indeed, did stumble, yet she did not fall. In other words, while the Hebrew nation failed in her calling, she, nevertheless, does not qualify as apostate!

Furthermore, he wrote that, **"if their rejection be the reconciliation of the world, what will their acceptance be but life from the
dead?"** (Rom 11:15) Not only does the apostle re-establish the
divine purpose behind Israel's rejection, which served God's plan to
reach the heathen nations of the world through the Messiah, he also
presents a very significant question, **"What will their acceptance be?"**
Obviously, Paul not only fully expected a future healing and acceptance for Israel, he also seemed to understand this national salvation
as a miracle which will benefit others as well. He answers his own
question, declaring that Israel's acceptance will mean nothing less
than **"life from the dead"**!

Purposefully the apostle uses such forceful language. He, in fact,
declares that Israel's acceptance by God will result in nothing less
than **resurrection life** impacting the entire world! He prophesies that
if the Jew being rejected led to the Gentile being accepted, what will
occur in God's divine plan when **the rejected Jew is rejected no
more?** Paul declares, it will mean resurrection life itself!

Significantly, the theme of the resurrection of the dead crowns
the revelation of many Old Testament prophets as they looked
ahead to the end of the age. The same promise is emphasized by the
Lord Jesus Himself and is foundational in the apostolic teachings!
We find it of great significance that the hope of the resurrection of
the dead is directly linked to Israel's ultimate spiritual healing and
restoration.

In addition, we know that the dead shall rise at the last trumpet,
which also will signify the return of the Lord to this realm (1 Thess
4:16). Therefore, it can be said that the restoration of Israel, the
resurrection of the dead, and the return of the Lord all join into one
apocalyptic and awesome climax of events. And while we do not
know whether these glorious events will happen simultaneously or
over a period of time, we understand that they are all interrelated
and triggered by the increase and nearing of His presence.

We fully expect this to happen. As the nation of Israel gradually
and painfully re-enters the embrace of God, His deposit of divine
life is increasingly unleashed upon all nations. As recent history
testifies, the unprecedented spread of the gospel throughout the
world in our century alone is intimately linked with the restoration
of the Jewish people, as a nation, to their land. Thus, Israel's resto-

ration serves as a catalyst in God's plan for end-time blessings, glory and harvest, as **life will surely triumph over death.**

Could it be that Satan understands God's purpose for Israel better than most Christians do? Is it possible that the endless conflicts surrounding Israel's restoration directly relate to and stem from the spiritual realities attached to that restoration? Indeed, it appears that the answer to both questions is "yes."

13

Time
to Restore

In considering the timing of the Lord and our proximity to the last days, we are very mindful of the hope which burned through past Christian generations. In each of these generations, there was a radical, prophetic-minded remnant who were convinced they were living at the end of the age. These saints interpreted the "evil man" of their generation to be the Antichrist, understood their particular hardships to be the great tribulation, and fully expected to witness the return of the Lord.

All of these precious saints were wrong; they died in their doctrinal error while holding onto their hope. **But yet, they were right!** They were right in their belief that they must prepare for the end-times and for the return of the Lord Jesus. And it is because of their zeal and prophetic fervor that the baton of faith and hope was handed down from generation to generation.

Considering this, how can we be certain that we are living in the last days? Could it be that we, too, are misinterpreting and exaggerating the prophetic signs of our days? Possibly so! However, we have something that none of the previous generations had. We have the resurrected and restored nation of Israel, which is without doubt the most significant sign of our times! The question then arises; is this really the time of Israel's final restoration?

The Lord's Timing

In searching the scriptures for clues as to our chronological position in God's overall plan, we come upon a number of prophetic predictions containing the word **"until"** which provide a sense of timing for our discussion. As Peter was testifying to the crowd in Jerusalem, he cried out, **"Repent therefore and return, that your sins may be wiped away, in order that times of refreshing may come from the presence of the Lord; and that He may send Jesus, the Christ appointed for you, whom heaven must receive UNTIL the period of restoration of all things about which God spoke by the mouth of His holy prophets from ancient time"** (Acts 3:19-21, emphasis mine). Our first "until" is found in these words.

An honest look at Peter's plea reveals a few important facts. First, he assures this Jewish multitude that refreshing times will come to them after they repent and turn to the Lord. Secondly, he declares that Jesus, the Messiah, is appointed for them. Thirdly, he emphasizes that heaven, as it were, is holding Jesus back from returning to earth right now, or as another translation reads, **"whom heaven must contain"** until the period of restoration of all things spoken by the ancient prophets.

Thus, we are given to understand that the return of the Lord (the end of this age) is awaiting this period of restoration. Therefore, we ask: what were these things of which the prophets prophesied to be restored? What was the emphasis of their prophetic vision into the future?

A simple review of the messages of restoration spoken of by the Old Testament prophets clearly shows that nearly all of their prophetic expectations were focused on the restoration of Israel at the end of this age. They proclaimed that the people will be restored to the land, their hearts will be restored to God, worship will be restored in the streets of Jerusalem, and the land itself will be restored to fruitfulness.

Indeed, it appears that Jesus will continue to be "held back" from returning for His bride and inheritance **until** that period in which Israel tastes the restoring and healing move of God.

"Until" the Land is Desolate

After the prophet Isaiah had his life-changing encounter with the presence of the Lord in the temple, he was commissioned with a unique mission. He was told to **"Render the hearts of this people insensitive, their ears dull, and their eyes dim, lest they see ... hear ... understand ... and return and be healed"** (Is 6:10). Indeed, this was a strange calling which can only be understood in light of God's purpose for Israel to be rejected for the sake of the Gentile nations.

Isaiah, who understood the prophetic weight of his call, replied, **"Lord, how long?"** (Is 6:11) He was not questioning God's action, but rather inquiring how long Israel would be left on the "back shelf," untouched and unhealed, while God's redeeming graces continue to sweep the nations? And the Lord answered, **"UNTIL cities are devastated and without inhabitant, houses are without people, and the land is utterly desolate, the Lord has removed men far away, and the forsaken places are many in the midst of the land"** (Is 6:11-12, emphasis mine). Here we find our second "until."

How long will Israel remain blind and deaf? How long will God's ancient people be held back from fully comprehending and embracing His divine purpose for them? How long before He can restore them back? The answer is, "until" the land of Israel has fully absorbed God's judgments!

This "until" has been fully satisfied. History testifies, as we present in chapter 16, of the utter devastation and rejection that the land of Israel has been under for millenniums. The land laid unloved, uncultivated and uncared for, losing vitality with each passing century as the succession of conquering armies raped her treasures time and time again.

My own family records testify concerning the early years of this century when my pioneering grandparents came into the land of promise, now filled with swamps, malaria and ruins. There was nothing left of the ancient glory and fruitfulness! Indeed, the second **"until"** had been thoroughly fulfilled, and it was time to rebuild.

"Until" Jerusalem is Free

As the Lord Jesus prophesied over Jerusalem, predicting her destruction which was soon to come and warning her inhabitants to flee, He finished with these words: **"And they will fall by the edge of the sword, and will be led captive into all the nations; and Jerusalem will be trampled underfoot by the Gentiles UNTIL the times of the Gentiles [nations] be fulfilled"** (Luke 21:24, emphasis mine). This is the third "until" we will consider.

One can say that the Lord Jesus was speaking both of Jerusalem's imminent destruction and of her future restoration in the same breath. With a sweeping prophetic declaration, the Lord predicted that as Israel is led into captivity, Jerusalem will continue under foreign heathen domination for a long time. And exactly how long a period would that be? When could the banner of shame, exile and slavery be removed? The Lord Himself answers that question, saying it will not end **"UNTIL the times of the Gentiles be fulfilled,"** and Jerusalem is no longer trampled under their feet.

This "until" was fulfilled in June of 1967, when the old city of Jerusalem was liberated in one swift strike of the Israeli defense forces during the Six-Day War. In fact, Israel was not planning to take Jerusalem at all during that war, and would have preferred to keep the eastern front with Jordan quiet and aggression-free. However, King Hussein of Jordan initiated fighting, and within a few days Israel was in possession of Judea, Samaria, and the whole city of Jerusalem! That day marked a significant change in the heavenlies, as Jerusalem exited out of that prophetic season which Jesus identified as **"the times of the Gentiles."**

Of course, God is still concerned with the nations of the world. Of course, He brings a harvest for Himself from every tribe, tongue, people and nation. However, the restoration of Israel has taken one more step forward as Jerusalem was recaptured after nearly 2000 years, and the third **"until"** was satisfied.

"Until" the People Bow

Through His tears the Lord Jesus again prophesied over Jerusalem, expressing His great passion to gather her children to Himself. Yet, facing their unbelief and denial, He cried out, **"For I** say to you, from now on you shall not see Me UNTIL you say, 'Blessed is He who comes in the name of the Lord!' " (Matt 23:39, emphasis mine); thus our fourth "until."

The Lord, being full of the Spirit, knew of the centuries filled with suffering and reproach which would come upon the Jews. He saw the long valley of the shadow of death Israel would have to pass through. But He also saw the end of it all, predicting that He would remain hidden from their sight UNTIL they lift up their hearts with faith and gratitude toward God. This "until" is being fulfilled in our days.

Though we expect that one day all of Israel will acknowledge God, we already see the beginnings of that miracle today. All throughout the land of Israel, dozens of indigenous Israeli congregations are standing as a prophetic witness, raising the cry, **"blessed is He who comes in the name of the Lord."**

With their hands lifted up and their hearts ablaze, this precious body of Israeli believers testifies today of the coming harvest of the whole nation. Thus, the question of "how long will Israel's blindness last" is being satisfied these very days in this **"until."**

"Until" the Fulness Comes

In Paul's writings, as well, we find a clear sense of God's timing. Nearing the end of his discourse to the Roman disciples, explaining the mystery of Israel's calling, rejection and restoration, he writes, **"For I do not want you, brethren, to be uninformed of this mystery, lest you be wise in your own estimation, that a partial hardening has happened to Israel UNTIL the fulness of the Gentiles [nations] has come in"** (Rom 11:25, emphasis mine). Here is our fifth "until."

Paul makes it exceedingly clear that only a partial hardening has happened to Israel, and that it will last only UNTIL the coming fulness of the Gentiles. We ask, therefore, what is that fulness, and is it already upon us? Is it now time for that partial hardening to be removed from Israel?

First, we know that the fulness of the Gentiles, or nations, corresponds to their full number. The NIV translation reads, **"until the full number of the Gentiles has come in."** And indeed, we believe that God's plan to heal and redeem Israel is directly related to the quantitative value of the harvest. God has a book and a pen, and He writes down the names of the redeemed. And as their full number comes in, His attention increasingly focuses upon Israel once again.

Secondly, the fulness of the Gentile nations undoubtedly corresponds with the overflowing cup of iniquities of the ungodly. When God spoke to Father Abraham concerning the return of his descendants from Egypt to their promised land, He said, **"Then in the fourth generation they shall return here, for the iniquity of the Amorite is not yet complete"** (Gen 15:16). In other words, the sinfulness and wickedness of the Amorites had not yet reached its fulness; thus, judgment could not yet be released! Likewise, at the end of this age there will come a time when even our God, in His great mercies and long-suffering, will say, **"no more!"** The cup of wickedness overflows, the sinfulness of the nations has reached its fulness, and judgment cannot be delayed.

Thirdly, the fulness of the Gentiles speaks of the blessed promise of the fulness of God's Spirit in His church. The prophesied maturing of the saints and perfecting of the bride of Christ will be characterized by a fulness of the Spirit and the virtue of the Lord Jesus Himself among the godly. Thus, His church from among the nations of the earth must reach a fulness without which Israel will not attain her own promised fulness. Indeed, the fulness of the Gentiles is coming in these very days, and the fifth **"until"** is on its way to fulfillment.

Thus, the times of the "untils" are upon us. The ancient prophecies concerning Israel's restoration are being fulfilled; the land has been thoroughly devastated and is being rebuilt. Jerusalem is no longer under foreign domination. The body of Messiah in Israel is proclaiming **"blessed is He who comes in the name of the Lord,"** and the fulness of the nations is coming in. Indeed, we are in the last days, and God's mighty hand is moving us closer each day to the culmination of our age.

The final and possibly the most profound "until" was spoken in Micah's prophecy. As the prophetic revelation concerning the advent of the incarnation of God's Son unfolds, and the Messiah's eternal glory is unveiled, the prophet continues, **"Therefore, He will give them [the sons of Israel] up UNTIL the time when she who is in labor has borne a child. Then the remainder of His brethren [the**

Gentile disciples] **will return to the sons of Israel"** (Micah 5:3, emphasis mine).

Indeed, Israel will be given up until the time of that great joining together of Jew and Gentile in the **one new man!**

14

What Will Their Acceptance Be?

This understanding of Israel's restoration as the harbinger of the broader restoration God will pour over all humanity finds confirmation in Paul's words that **"the spiritual is not first, but the natural; then the spiritual"** (1 Cor 15:46). And this truth, indeed, is found in all levels of creation—from Adam to Christ, from our natural birth to our spiritual birth and from Israel to the church. The natural always precedes the spiritual.

Recent history provides us with clear demonstrations of these dynamics of restoration and healing as they start in the natural realm and overflow to find their ultimate fulfillment in the spiritual. In this century alone, we have witnessed the resurrection of the nation of Israel from the grave of exile and genocide. Few other nations can claim or prove a recorded national lineage which spans so many thousands of years. And while some nations possess an ancient historical background, it is chiefly cultural in nature. Israel's heritage, however, is a clear demonstration of an uninterrupted ancient national identity with undeniable geographic claims.

Such a phenomenon of a national resurrection is unquestionably supernatural, and in order to gain understanding we must direct our search toward the purposes and promises of God. His Word alone is responsible for the preserving of Israel throughout 2,500 years of captivity and exile; His Word alone is also responsible for her present restoration.

This national restoration of the people to their land has a spiritual counterpart. We find that for every move of God toward ethnic Israel there has been a subsequent move of God toward the church. Indeed, each time the Holy Spirit moved in the natural arena, He also moved in the spiritual. Let us consider the witness of history:

The Regathering, 1897:

Dr. Theodore Herzl convened the first international Zionist conference in Basal, Switzerland, thus officially birthing the Zionist movement. This was a most unusual, even supernatural, movement among the Jewish people, inspiring their gathering together and returning to the land they left 1,800 years earlier. In a most incredible fashion and against great opposition, this dispersed people, devoid of government, economy, or territorial integrity, rose as a corpse rises from its grave.

At that point, the early immigration had already been underway for a number of years, and into the land then called Palestine came wave after wave of Jewish pioneers, among them my own grandparents. The territory they found and began to cultivate and populate was mostly desolate, unloved and undeveloped. The countryside was covered with swamps and infested with malaria, cloaked in the shame and barrenness of centuries of neglect; Jerusalem herself was no more than a half-ruined village.

In his hotel room, Herzl recorded in his diary, "Today, in Basal, I created the Jewish state!" And when we consider the secular background and political motives of this great man, we can better appreciate the prophetic mantle God sovereignly placed upon him for this task. He truly served the purposes of God as a prophet, speaking words of life and direction to a nation yet unborn.

Significantly, nearly fifty years after this prophetic declaration in his hotel room, Israel became a sovereign state!

Thus, the end of the nineteenth century and the beginning of the twentieth century marked the birthing of the movement that restored the people to the land.

The Parallel:

Almost to the year, as the Zionist movement gained global recognition and velocity, God also moved upon the church. Hunger for His presence drove pockets of Christians to their knees seeking Him. Heaven responded, and Topeka, Kansas (1900), Azuza Street (1903), Chile, China, and other recorded locations worldwide all experienced a tremendous outpouring. God's Spirit fell mightily and remained long enough to birth the Pentecostal movement—a sweeping holy wind that encircled the globe many times, yielding a harvest of nearly three hundred million born-again believers. Indeed, as natural Israel began her restoration to the Promised Land, spiritual Israel was being restored to her inheritance as well.

The Tongue:

As few realize, the Hebrew language became dormant for nearly two millenniums. During this season of exile, the mother tongue was practiced only by rabbis and teachers, and even then just during religious duties and synagogue services. In the early years of the twentieth century, parallel to the increased immigration of Jewish pioneers into the land, a man named Eliezer Ben-Yehuda (son of Judah) set himself to singlehandedly restore the ancient Hebrew tongue.

History tells of his indescribable zeal and unwavering commitment to this monumental task. Days and nights, working ceaselessly with great personal loss and sacrifice, this zealot restored the language of the Bible to the people of the Bible. His own family underwent mockery and persecution as he insisted they speak only Hebrew in the midst of a Jewish population who spoke anything but Hebrew. His sacrifice and effort produced the desired fruit, and Hebrew once again became the official language spoken by the Jewish people in their land.

The Parallel:

The restoration of the gift of tongues to the church, together with other spiritual gifts, came simultaneously. As part of the divine package during the Pentecostal awakening in the early years of this century, tongues were restored to a fuller measure. After centuries of limited expression, as was the case with Israel's natural tongue, now spiritual Israel also rediscovered a long-lost treasure with its benefits and accompanying edification (1 Cor 14:4). And while we understand that the gift of tongues is not essential for salvation, nor does it guarantee that a person is "filled with the Spirit," we recognize the historical progression as God works in both the natural and spiritual levels of fulfillment.

Statehood, 1948:

Delivered by Britain from the Moslem Turkish Empire that was by nature hostile to the purposes of God, the land continued to be painfully reclaimed by Jewish settlers.

Dr. Weizmann, a Jewish scientist serving the British Defense Department, gained England's gratitude for his wartime invention of a new explosive that turned the tide against the Germans during World War I. When asked for recompense he responded, "I ask for a national home for my people in their ancient land."

Through much political maneuvering and with strong support from godly British statesmen, England granted his request and was commissioned by the League of Nations to administrate Palestine in preparation for the establishment of a Jewish state. However, politics are often corrupt and the increasing need for oil among the industrial nations further tainted the British conscience. Looking with favor toward the Arab oil-producing nations, England's policy in the region underwent great changes, openly discriminating against the Jewish population, and the embryo of the state of Israel was almost aborted!

After years of struggle against both Arab hostilities and British oppression, Israel was founded, and in 1948 received international recognition as a sovereign Jewish state. This act was immediately followed by the War of Independence which was forced upon her by five neighboring Arab armies. The national life, which had emerged fifty years earlier and was now properly established in the national homeland, was again threatened with extinction. Yet, as the Lord spoke, **"I will restore the captivity of My people Israel, and they will rebuild the ruined cities and live in them ... I will also plant them on their land and they will not again be rooted out from their land which I have given them"** (Amos 9:14-15).

The Parallel:
The late 1940s and the early 1950s marked the emergence of major powerful and international ministries; some of them are still with us today serving the nations. These anointed vessels helped shape our present Christianity and mobilized God's people worldwide. Revelation increased, miracles were restored, and the five-fold ministry anointings—the ascension gifts—were rediscovered. Indeed, as the Lord was unfolding His plan of restoration in establishing Israel's statehood, so the church was being restored, increasing in power and order.

Jerusalem, 1967:
Again Israel was forced into another conflict and the Six-Day (miraculous) War broke out. Hostile armies pressed hard from both the Egyptian and Syrian borders, and the fighting was intense. The Israeli government genuinely desired to keep the long eastern front with Jordan aggression-free, so that combat efforts could concentrate on the Egyptian and Syrian fronts. In fact, a message was sent from Jerusalem to King Hussein of Jordan stating, "If you don't shoot, we won't shoot."

But the king succumbed to the pressure of his Arab neighbors, and made the mistake of ordering his forces into action. Fierce fighting ensued over the eastern front, centering mostly around the Jerusalem area, and two days later the city of Jerusalem was liberated by Israeli paratroopers who broke in through the Lion's Gate. **After 2,500 years of oppression and foreign domination, the whole of Jerusalem was again in Jewish hands!**

It seems that every empire which ever existed under the sun has believed it was divinely commissioned to conquer and rule over Jerusalem. The Babylonians, Medes, Greeks, Romans, Spaniards, Arabs, Turks, British and others attempted to rule over this city, raping and desecrating her treasures, until she became a ravaged, desolate, and flea-infested ruin! Through Zechariah God spoke these sobering words, **"I scattered them with a storm wind among all the nations whom they have not known. Thus the land is desolated behind them, so that no one went back and forth, for they made the pleasant land desolate"** (Zech 7:14).

However, as it has been said, "Jerusalem is the city where empires are buried." All these world powers came and left this city, their memory preserved only in such things as historic archives, architecture, and the arts, while Jerusalem still stands!

June 1967 marked the end of her shame. Indeed, the Lord Jesus prophesied that **"Jerusalem will be trampled under foot by the Gentiles until the times of the Gentiles be fulfilled"** (Luke 21:24). And thus, before the world's eyes, the progressive restoration of Israel took another giant step forward as the national capital was now restored to the national homeland.

The Parallel:
The late 1960s marked the beginning of what we call the charismatic movement. The fire of God swiftly spread throughout Christendom, leaping over denominational and traditional barriers, penetrating into every stream and movement. Overnight one could find charismatic Catholics, Baptists, Anglicans, Mennonites, Lutherans, and many others. God created an awesome, common denominator throughout the whole of His body on earth as He sent the fire of His Spirit! And though the charismatic movement has given way to other subsequent waves of God's healing and restoration, it provided another significant layer in the renewal and re-establishing of biblical truths as present reality.

The Exodus from the Soviet Union:
Massive Jewish emigration from the Soviet Bloc began in the late 1980s, which resulted in more than half a million Russian Jewish immigrants added to Israel's population, a sudden and shocking growth of about fifteen percent! This miraculous release of the Russian Jews, still continuing, was initiated unexpectedly following decades of Communist oppression which kept its subjects imprisoned.

Of course, it was the hand of the Lord falling upon Communism which unlocked the gates of this political prison, thus adding another essential ingredient to the fulfillment of His Word concerning Israel's restoration. It was the prophet Jeremiah who spoke of these distant events, saying, " **'behold, days are coming,' declares the Lord, 'when it will no longer be said, "As the Lord lives, who brought up the sons of Israel out of the land of Egypt," but, "as the Lord lives, who brought up the sons of Israel from the land of the north and from all the countries where He had banished them." For I will restore them to their own land which I gave to their fathers' "** (Jer 16:14-15).

The Parallel:
Almost simultaneously and immediately following the release of the Russian Jewish population, we witnessed a massive spread of the gospel in that same region, so spiritually deprived for so long. Western missionaries, evangelists, massive crusades, and leadership training seminars are not only permitted, but oftentimes requested, in the former Soviet Union. Indeed, the "natural exodus" immediately preceded a "spiritual exodus" for multitudes who now follow the "greater Moses" beyond the bondage and slavery of the prince of this world.

Ultimate Healing

These powerful parallels are obvious. Progressive steps of healing and restoration occurred simultaneously with the natural and the spiritual seed. And while our God is not a science, nor His ways exact formulas, still these historic evidences demand that we too, like Paul, should ask, **"What will their FULL acceptance be?"**

If the emergence of the national Israeli embryo (1900) paralleled the powerful Pentecostal wave, if the restoration of the national sovereignty (1948) paralleled power and revelation ministries, and if the recapturing of the national capital, Jerusalem, (1967) paralleled the charismatic outpouring of God's Spirit, **"How much more will their fulfillment be!"** (Rom 11:12)

What will it be like when all of Israel, from the Red Sea to the Upper Galilean Peaks, is sovereignly transformed into one colossal upper room? What will it be like when **"the Spirit of grace and of**

supplication" (Zech 12:10) is poured out in national dimensions as promised, birthing deep grief and true national repentance? What will the parallel work of the Lord be, in and through the church at that hour, but **"life from the dead"?** Healing, restoration, resurrection, and the ultimate reconciliation of man and of creation back to God will have been accomplished!

What will **their** full acceptance mean? Nothing less than **our** full acceptance! The two, Jew and Gentile, shall fully become **"one new man"** in the midst of much turmoil and on the threshold of glory. Thus shall the Father's heart be satisfied and the scripture fulfilled that says, **"And all these** [the Hebrew forerunners] **having gained approval through their faith, did not receive what was promised, because God had provided something better for us, so that apart from us they should not be made perfect"** (Heb 11:39-40).

15

First Fruits

First the Natural

The scriptures testify that **"the spiritual is not first, but the natural; then the spiritual"** (1 Cor 15:46). The great and sovereign move of restoration, which is powerfully impacting both the Jewish people and the nations of the world, indeed, started in the natural.

The physical regathering of the Jewish people gained momentum during the late 1800s and the early 1900s. A human flood began sweeping from the four corners of the earth, carrying multitudes of Jews to their ancient homeland. Whole communities were uprooted, at times violently, as this great national upheaval redefined the destiny of the Jewish people.

I remember the stories of my grandparents who left Russia just prior to the rise of Communism, traveling to what was then called Palestine. Leaving behind possessions, careers and identity, they gave up all to gain the promise. Forgotten scriptures were coming alive and ancient prophecies were thrust to the forefront of global affairs.

And indeed, this physical gathering continues to this very day, as we watch with awe prophecy after prophecy being fulfilled to the letter. It was through Isaiah that the Spirit of the Lord promised, **"Do not fear, for I am with you; I will bring your offspring from the east, and gather you from the west. I will say to the north, 'Give them up!' And to the south, 'Do not hold them back.' Bring My sons from afar, and My daughters from the ends of the earth"** (Is 43:5-6). Thus, the return of the Ethiopian Jewish community, the ongoing exodus out of the former Soviet Union, and the constant trickle of Jewish immigration from around the world, all testify to the ongoing fulfillment of this prophecy.

However, the natural dimensions of this awesome work of restoration, encompassing the regathering of the people, the re-establishing of the state, and the maintenance of territorial integrity, are but the beginning. The promises pertaining to the spiritual restoration of Israel have yet to be realized—a fulfillment which, in fact, has already begun.

We read in Ezekiel's prophecy that the natural healing of the nation will precede the spiritual healing. The prophet describes a people who are first gathered from the four corners of the earth, then established within their ancient land, claiming and cultivating it, and only then will they be spiritually revived. **"For I will take you from the nations, gather you from all the lands, and bring you into your own land. THEN I will sprinkle clean water on you . . . I will cleanse you . . . I will give you a new heart . . . a new spirit . . . and I will put My Spirit within you"** (Ez 36:24-27, emphasis mine). This term "then" is the line drawn between the natural and spiritual revivals—the hinge upon which the ancient gates will swing, ushering in Israel's ultimate healing.

After prophesying in bold terms of the restoration of the people to the land, the prophet declares that "then" the spiritual work will begin! Only "then" will clean water be sprinkled, a new heart given, and God's Spirit restored to the nation. Indeed, first comes the restoration to the land; then follows the restoration in the land! Even as it is written, **first comes the natural, then the spiritual.**

The Israeli Body of Believers

As we observe the unfolding of God's prophetic Word over the nation of Israel and the Jewish people, we do so with the understanding that no man ever successfully predicted or interpreted these prophecies before their actual fulfillment. It is a biblical and historical fact **"that no prophecy of Scripture is a matter of one's own interpretation"** (2 Peter 1:20). Rather, it is in the context of the **fulfillment** of prophecies that the human witness arises declaring, "this is that which was spoken of by the prophets."

For example, the manifestation of the Eternal Lamb of God in the person of the Messiah was missed by most of His contemporaries in spite of the numerous prophecies pointing to His coming and His ministry. Yet this revelation was widely received **after** the fact of His death, burial and resurrection. Having seen the scriptures fulfilled, and being enlightened by the Spirit, both the disciples and the multitudes who joined them could now see the revelation and properly interpret the prophecy.

In light of that, as we observe the ongoing progress and growth of the Israeli body of believers in the last generation, we, too, are saying, "This is that which was spoken of by the prophets." Ezekiel promised a spiritual cleansing and, indeed, we see the beginning of its fulfillment in the cleansing and infilling of the emerging Israeli congregations. Throughout the land of Israel, one can find maturing disciples growing in Christlikeness and devotion to God. This which was promised for Israel on a national scale has already begun to dawn in the Israeli body of believers. Let us never despise nor neglect the day of small beginnings!

Indeed, as Paul prophesied, **"And they also, if they do not continue in their unbelief, will be grafted in; for God is able to graft them in again . . . into their own olive tree"** (Rom 11:23-24).

The Israeli church and other communities of Messianic Jews around the world testify to the beginning of this "grafting in" which is promised. Indeed, prophecy is in the process of fulfillment, and the redemption of Israel should no longer be viewed as a futuristic event which we anticipate by faith. Rather, this redemption has already begun and is to be accepted as a present reality to which we commit, not only by faith but in deed!

In the course of our labors in Israel during the late 1970s and 1980s, we were blessed and privileged to witness and participate in the emerging of local bodies of believers that quickly spread throughout the nation. Hebrew-speaking congregations were successfully planted, often by a miraculous and sovereign work of the Holy Spirit, and the spiritually darkened landscape was dotted with lights.

However, it is important to remember that there was a valid Christian witness and presence in Israel prior to that period. In our century alone, practically every mainline denomination established beachheads in what was called the "Holy Land," erecting church buildings and providing Christian shelters in key locations. These labors, although faithful and earnest, rarely penetrated the human fabric of the emerging nation, and brought very little fruit. It was not yet the timing of the Lord.

A new grace and fresh anointing were granted us in Israel in the late 1970s. This anointing was for the purpose of establishing local Israeli congregations and defining their character and vision. Instead of foreign missions and denominational workers, the Spirit was now calling forth the local indigenous body.

After years of tenacious intercession and intense longing, this anointing came to groups of young Israelis. We were moved to breakthrough after breakthrough in the areas of worship, intercession, unity, warfare, and church government. For a few years it seemed as though there was more life being poured from heaven than the earthen vessels could contain. Truly, after nearly 1,800 years of absence, a viable and fruitful believing community was reborn, sinking her roots deep into the fabric of the nation.

In less than a decade, we witnessed the Lord casting people as seed, establishing congregations throughout the land of Israel. Today, in every metropolitan area, in some of the small communities and in many rural regions, we can easily find bold and precious groups of disciples—some numbering in the hundreds, others merely a family or two. Most congregations are led by an eldership patterned after the biblical model, with the five-fold ministries of Ephesians 4:11 gradually and tenderly being restored, as the Lord gives grace. These indigenous congregations are almost forty in number at the time of this writing. Some of these precious groups own a meeting hall, some rent, while others meet in homes.

Statistically, the numbers of known born-again believers in Israel increased by nearly 2000 percent during the last decade or so! The Israeli church multiplied itself by nearly twenty times in ten years, possibly qualifying to be called the fastest-growing church in the world! And yet, one needs to understand that the believing community in Israel is still but a tiny fraction of the total population.

Young Israeli men and women, some of them former "rejects" of society, have been drawn to the love of the Father through true revelation of the work and person of Messiah. Many of these are presently serving on the cutting edge of the purposes of God in Israel. Some, burning with a prophetic zeal, are ministering to the Lord and to the body; some are anointed and commissioned as full-time evangelists, inspiring and equipping the saints; some are shepherds of the flock, elders who sit in the gates, faithfully serving the endless needs of the growing congregations.

This new generation is constantly standing in the gap, interceding and travailing for the rest of the nation. These disciples understand the prophetic moving of the Lord in a very instinctive and "down-to-earth" manner, as they live amidst fulfilled prophecies. These young congregations and ministries fully realize that they are first fruits, standing in faith and in warfare on behalf of the rest of the harvest!

The battle, indeed, is fierce. The veil of many centuries of blindness, grief and unbelief is not easily removed. Waves of persecution break out throughout the land at times, leaving behind slashed tires, burned meeting halls, unemployed saints who lose jobs because of their faith, and various other forms of harassment, mostly from fanatic and militant orthodox factions. And, in addition to the natural struggles, this young body of believers absorbs heavy and constant spiritual assault as they stand as a buffer, in Christ, between the forces of evil and the nation of Israel.

Indeed, quite a church this is! These are our Israeli friends and comrades we left behind when the Lord called us to the United States. And, in addition to providing financial support for many of them through the generous donations of Christians in the West, we see these dear ones twice a year as we bring in teams of intercessors to pray over the land and over the body of believers spread throughout the country. Truly, it is not only our joy but also an honor for us to witness and to participate in the moving of God's hand throughout Israel as He rebuilds the ancient ruins, heals the land itself, and prepares the nation for His last and final visitation.

16

The Poor in
Jerusalem

"For Macedonia and Achaia have been pleased to make a contribution for the poor among the saints in Jerusalem. Yes, they were pleased to do so, and they are indebted to them. For if the Gentiles have shared in their spiritual things, they are indebted to minister to them also in material things" (Rom 15:26-27).

It is important to understand that Paul's admonition to the Roman disciples concerning the Gentile **indebtedness** to the Jewish brethren was not a one-time flash of sentiment or a regional issue only. Historical facts support the understanding that, from the time of the early apostles to Constantine and the first Catholic pope, the church throughout Asia Minor and Europe was engaged in a steady flow of giving toward the saints in Judea.

Even more, we read that while the prophetic Word in Acts, chapter 11, indicated **"that there would certainly be a great famine all over the world"** (Acts 11:28), the response of the brethren in Antioch was that **"in the proportion that any of the disciples had**

means, each of them determined to send a contribution for the relief of the brethren living in Judea" (Acts 11:29). Surely, many other needy congregations throughout the region could have benefited from Antioch's support at that time. However, there appears to be a clear recognition that the brethren in Judea should still receive special relief from the Gentile congregations.

Apparently, this tradition of giving to the Jewish brethren in the ancient homeland was a recognizable and ongoing apostolic tradition. Therefore, we speak not only of a donation to a poor or needy community—there are many of those throughout the world. Rather, we speak of a spiritual obligation of the Gentile branches to their Jewish brethren who preceded them in God's olive tree.

This precious apostolic tradition, though already on the decline, existed for many years. It was the power-hungry second pope who officially cut off all financial aid to the saints in Jerusalem. He did so because he feared the descendants of the original disciples, still living and ministering in Israel, would retain church authority which he wanted exclusively in Rome (from the writings of Malachi Martin, a Roman Catholic historian). Here surfaces that spiritual conflict between ancient Rome and Jerusalem, which may yet come to its final culmination at the closing of this age!

Tragically, from that point on, the Gentile church became more and more anti-Semitic in its policies and official pronouncements. One hundred years after the official severing of the Jewish believers from the nourishment of the body, the world plunged into a thousand years of spiritual darkness. Indeed, there is a direct correlation between the alienation of the Jewish brethren and the fallen spiritual condition of the church.

This drifting away from the early apostolic authority which kept the body moving by the Spirit of the Lord became evident in the latter years of Paul, Peter, Jude and John. Each of them warned not so much of the threat of the Judaizers as of the lawlessness emerging from within the ranks of the Gentile branches. Indeed, that drifting away from her roots cost the church unimaginable disasters and many wasted centuries.

The Gentiles have been the majority in the body of Christ for so long that history has clouded our perspective, hiding from us the truth that **"the Gentiles have shared in their [the Jews] spiritual** things" (Rom 15:27). The fact is that the gospel and the revelation of Jesus Himself came to the Gentiles via Jerusalem, thus introducing multitudes of heathen into the spiritual commonwealth of Israel. Therefore, it is our conviction that as the church recognizes and embraces these truths, her healing and restoration will speedily come from the Lord. It is because of this **biblical spiritual debt** that the Gentile branches are **"indebted to minister to them** [the Jewish brethren] **also in material things"** (Rom 15:27).

The Plan is the Man

While there has been some recognition of that **indebtedness**, we can say with certainty that much of the giving toward Israel has been somewhat "starry-eyed" and unrealistic. Those segments of the church who engage in supporting "the Israeli cause" oftentimes fail to distinguish between sentimental commitment toward traditional Judaism, the secular state of Israel, and God's heart toward the living body of believers in that land. Because there is so much fascination among Christians with the rebuilding of the temple in Jerusalem, many reach into their pockets to support Orthodox Judaism while being absolutely ignorant of the existence of the "living temple" being built there these very days.

The encouragement and enablement from the church toward the Israeli brethren must be expressed through intercession, travail, **and** financial support for the saints. The growing body of believers in Israel is at the eye of the greatest spiritual "hurricane" our world will ever know. This emerging Israeli church stands as first fruits of the whole nation and as the spearhead of the Lord's awesome work in the region. Truly, in these congregations are embodied both the promises for the national redemption with its worldwide effects and the intense warfare surrounding it.

As more and more segments of the body of Christ open up to this revelation, it is necessary to correct a common mistake. It has been the policy of some to support God's moving in Israel by "assistance only through our representatives." In other words, foreign missionaries, programs, and cultural procedures are imported from other lands. And though often done unintentionally, this particular attitude of "going in like gangbusters to Israel to convert the Jews" is arrogant, unbiblical, and has brought nothing but disastrous results.

The fact is that the scriptures clearly identify a unique ministry to the Jewish people that should be recognized in its specific characteristics. There are distinctive anointings designed especially for the Jewish people. Even Paul, in speaking of his affirmation by the eldership in Jerusalem, said that he **"had been entrusted with the gospel to the uncircumcised [Gentile], just as Peter had been to the circumcised [Jew]"** (Gal 2:7).

There is, indeed, a distinct difference of anointing between those sent to reach the heathen nations and those sent to restore the Jewish nation. Thus, in speaking of our moral and scriptural obligation to **"minister to them also in material things,"** we recognize that our support belongs with those to whom the **gospel of the circumcision** has been committed.

As the Lord spoke to our hearts that **the plan is the man,** we found that the most effective assistance we can offer is in supporting people rather than projects or programs. God's anointing and blessing will always focus on the right person with the right heart in the right position, rather than on programs and property. Thus, it has been our endeavor to free some of God's ministers in Israel from the pressing need to provide for their households in the challenging Israeli economy, that they may devote themselves fully to the Lord.

Basic needs, transportation and housing are extremely expensive in Israel. Taxes are very high, as more than half the national budget goes to the defense ministry for security and military needs. Also, the massive emigration from the former Soviet Union is adding a challenging dimension to the existing difficulties. Housing, jobs, language, and social and cultural adjustments are but a few of these challenges.

With this in mind, it is fitting for the Gentile church to agree with and participate in this divine exchange, a transaction in which funds are both appointed and anointed for godly and timely purposes in Israel. Undoubtedly, this manner of giving constitutes a pleasing aroma before the Lord as we pray like Paul did, **"that my service for Jerusalem may prove acceptable to the saints"** (Rom 15:31).

There is a day coming when, in the context of Israel's regathering, this promise shall be fulfilled, **"Then you will see and be radiant, and your heart will thrill and rejoice; Because the abundance of the sea will be turned to you, the wealth of the nations will come to you"** (Is 60:5). And again, the prophetic Word promises that, **"You will eat the wealth of nations, and in their riches you will boast"** (Is 61:6). Indeed, we believe that while these promises do extend to include all of God's elect, their immediate scriptural object is the restored nation of Israel.

Until such a time as the Lord Himself sovereignly and miraculously brings economic relief and prosperity to Israel, **we must do our part!** As small or as large as our individual or corporate portion may be in this equation, we are assured that the Lord's pleasure and purpose is to sustain and build the Israeli church through the hands of the Gentile brethren. (We will be honored and happy to help guide your giving toward that end if you contact our office.)

SECTION FOUR:

The Struggle to Restore

Introduction

As is the case with every facet of life and creation, labor and travail will always accompany the coming forth of new life. And often it could be said that the greater the battle—the greater the gain!

Observing the animal kingdom, we find that the lower life forms usually give birth to the next generation easily and without complications. Consider the fly or the worm, for example. On the other hand, the higher and more complex the creature, the more risky and demanding is the birthing process. A bigger difference yet is found between the beasts that walk the earth and the birds that fly the sky.

Those destined to leave the earth and soar must go through the difficulty and struggle of forcing their way out of the eggshell or the cocoon which contained their previous form. In fact, any attempt to help ease their way out, to intervene by cracking the eggshell or slitting the cocoon for them, will always result in weakening the creature and damaging their ability to fulfill their own destiny. Thus, struggle is natural and necessary.

Considering the miraculous birthing of the nation of Israel and the cracking of a shell of blindness and isolation two thousand years old, we must expect resistance, hardship and warfare to accompany the event. Indeed, that warfare focuses on the issue of the land of Israel, the regathering of the people to the land in our century, and the spiritual awakening of the nation in that land.

17

The Battle
Over the Land

How simple it would be to analyze and define the mystery of the Jew if the issue could be limited to the mystical and spiritual realms alone. Books could be written, lectures given, and conferences held without ever having to apply our convictions in practical down-to-earth terms. In other words, if Israel was but a homeless people group and Jewishness only a religious culture, then one could relegate the issues to the abstract and ethereal realms. However, Israel is also a land—a very tangible piece of real estate in which dreams become reality, theological speculations translate into every-day facts, and spiritual aspirations take on a very authentic and practical image.

In Isaiah's vision of the approaching Messianic age, he wrote, **"Then it will happen on that day that the Lord will again recover the second time with His hand the remnant of His people, who will remain, from Assyria, Egypt, Pathros, Cush, Elam, Shinar, Hamath, and from the islands of the sea. And He will lift up a STANDARD** for the nations, and will assemble the banished ones of Israel, and will gather the dispersed of Judah from the four corners of the earth" (Is 11:11-12, emphasis mine).

Indeed, in preparation for the unfolding of the blessed Messianic reign of Jesus over the whole earth, Isaiah pinpoints the fact that the regathering of the Jewish people from the four corners of the earth is to serve as "a standard for the nations." Thus, on the threshold of the world's greatest spiritual awakening and conflict (which will characterize the last days), God has sovereignly placed this supernatural event, the regathering of Israel, to serve as a banner—a divine statement made to draw the attention of the nations and the affection of the church to the Lord's sovereignty and faithfulness.

Through Israel, God has set about to prove to an evil and unbelieving world the reality of His endless love and sovereign authority in the affairs of men and nations. The very fact that spiritual principles govern and determine political, economic and strategic developments in the Middle East today is divine evidence of the reality of God and His eternal plan.

Whose Land?

While much attention is rightfully drawn to the immediate issues concerning national claims to this territory by both Jews and Arabs, the issue does not start there. The origin of Israel's ownership goes deeper than history reveals or the human mind comprehends. The fact is that the land of Israel does not belong to any certain people group!

In Moses' prophetic warning, God was describing in detail Israel's calamity and great devastation when the people turn their backs on Him. And yet He said, "If they confess their iniquity and the iniquity of their forefathers . . . or if their uncircumcised heart becomes humbled . . . then I will remember My covenant with Jacob . . . Isaac . . . Abraham . . . and I will remember the LAND" (Lev 26:40-42, emphasis mine).

Here we see that prior to Israel's conquest of the Promised Land and before the establishment of a "national beachhead" in Canaan, God was already concerned about the land. He said that He will not only remember the people, the patriarchs and the covenants, but He "will remember the LAND."

What was it about this particular land that gave it such signifi-cance in the divine counsel of the Almighty who possesses the whole universe? Why such interest and commitment to this particular piece of real estate, so tiny and obscure?

Joel's prophecy offers a unique insight into this mystery: **"For behold, in those days and at that time, when I restore the fortunes of Judah and Jerusalem, I will gather all the nations, and bring them down to the valley of Jehoshaphat. Then I will enter into judg-ment with them there on behalf of My people and My inheritance, Israel, whom they have scattered among the nations; and they have divided up MY LAND"** (Joel 3:1-2, emphasis mine).

God, in this dramatic end-times scenario of judgment and justice, clearly identifies Himself with Israel as **"My people"** and **"My inheritance."** However, God's final indictment against the ungodly nations is that they have divided up **"My land."** Right here, in the clearest of terms, God defines the unquestionable ownership of the land of Israel. He says this land is **"My land."** Thus, many centuries after God promised the land to Abraham and his descendants, He still calls it **"My land,"** establishing and re-emphasizing His undeni-able claim of ownership to this territory.

Given To Whom?

The fact that the territory of ancient Canaan was promised in covenant to Abraham and His descendants through Isaac cannot be denied (see Gen 15:18; Gen 17:8,19-21; Gen 26:4).

In addition, the promise of Psalm 105 resounds with the depth of commitment and intensity which characterized the relationship God established between the people of Israel and the land of Israel. **"He has remembered His covenant forever, the word which He com-manded to a thousand generations, the covenant which He made with Abraham, and His oath to Isaac. Then He confirmed it to Jacob for a statute, to Israel as an everlasting covenant, saying, 'To you I will give the land of Canaan as the portion of your inheri-tance' "** (Psalm 105:8-11).

In these verses, the entrusting of the land to the nation of Israel is described in biblical and legal terms, carrying the full weight of God's eternal purpose. His **word, oath, statute and everlasting cove-nant** are all guarantees placed as guardians to preserve and protect the sanctity of this transaction. Thus, the inheritance God gave Israel in terms of territorial integrity is unquestionable and everlasting.

We cannot overemphasize the significance of these words. From God's perspective, that of the landlord, the territory was entrusted to a particular people. They were commanded to possess and dwell in that land only, and there to conduct their national life according to His statutes and commandments. **The land is God's!** Israel is legally unauthorized and forbidden to give it away, sell it or negotiate any part of it. Here again, the divine reality clashes head-on with political ambitions, human manipulations and demonic deceptions.

Though the land was given to Abraham's descendants through Isaac in covenant, there were conditions to their possession of the land. The scripture testifies that ancient Israel disqualified herself from the position of tending the land given her by God, and, as history unfolded, the nation was expelled and driven into exile. As prophesied, both the people and the territory entered a time of shame and desolation.

Indeed, the Jewish people were dispersed among the nations, there to live in perpetual fears, uncertainties, and persecutions for millenniums (Lev 26). The land also, according to the prophetic Word, was abandoned, forsaken and desolate. The various empires and conquerors occupying the region from A.D. 70 to 1948 never cared for it as their own. The land was greatly neglected and literally raped of its produce and resources, to the point that it became almost uninhabitable.

In 1835, a traveler by the name of Alphanso de Lamartine commented: "Outside the gates of Jerusalem we saw no living object, heard no living sound." Indeed, at that time, as it had been for centuries, Jerusalem was no more than a half-ruined, flea-infested village. Mark Twain visited the region in 1867 and described in his book, *The Innocents Abroad*: "A desolate country whose soil is rich enough, but is given wholly to weeds—a silent mournful expanse. We never saw a human being on the whole route."

Indeed, both the nation and the land incurred the curse of God during this extended season of reproach. The blessing was withdrawn, rainfall greatly diminished, and the land once flowing with milk and honey was now taken over by the sands blown in with the eastern winds from the Arabian Desert. And yet, the same scriptures that foretold of this calamity also gave hope for a future restoration, healing and fruitfulness.

Terms of Prosperity

Ezekiel, chapter 36, records a most unusual prophecy. God speaks directly to the actual landscape of Israel, saying, **"Therefore, O mountains of Israel, hear the word of the Lord God. Thus says the Lord God to the mountains and to the hills, to the ravines and to the valleys, to the desolate wastes and to the forsaken cities, which have become a prey and a derision to the rest of the nations which are round about . . . 'Surely in the fire of My jealousy I have spoken against the rest of the nations . . . who appropriated MY LAND for themselves as a possession with wholehearted joy and with scorn of soul' "** (Ez 36:4-5, emphasis mine). The Lord, while setting the stage for His future judgments (as in Joel's prophecy), again declares His ownership of the land by saying, "My land."

However, God's amazing Word to the very terrain of the land of Israel continues. **"But you, O mountains of Israel, you will put forth your branches and bear your fruit for My people Israel; for they will soon come. . . . and you shall be cultivated and sown. And I will multiply men on you, all the house of Israel"** (Ez 36:8-10).

Not only is the prophetic vision reaching forward thousands of years into the great regathering of our day, but the promise is given specifically for the land to be fruitful again. This fruitfulness, however, is exclusively and directly related to the return of the Jewish people to the land and their loving cultivation of it. **"Yes, I will cause men—My people Israel—to walk on you and possess you, so that you will become their inheritance and never again bereave them of children"** (Ez 36:12). The imagery of the people and the land carries the dynamics of passion, intimacy and interaction of husband and wife. Only at their coming together will they blossom and bear fruit again.

Incredible as it may seem, God continues to speak to His land, comforting her and promising healing and life. He not only defines the terms of the future fruitfulness and prosperity, but He continues to say to the soil, **" 'And I will not let you hear insults from the nations anymore, nor will you bear disgrace from the peoples any**

longer, nor will you cause your nation to stumble any longer,' declares the Lord God" (Ez 36:15). Can you hear the depth of passion
and tender care in God's heart toward His land? The Lord, in these
scriptures, is actually comforting, encouraging and giving hope to His
land and its mountains, valleys and plains.

Simultaneously, in the very same chapter, the prophetic Word
addresses the restoration of the people of Israel: "For I will take you
from the nations, gather you from all the lands, and bring you into
your own land. Then I will sprinkle clean water on you and you will
be clean; I will cleanse you from all your filthiness . . . I will give
you a new heart and put a new spirit within you . . . and I will put
My Spirit within you" (Ez 36:24-27).

The promise for the nation of Israel is that her spiritual restoration will surely take place, but only after her return to the land!
That mystical chemistry that only exists between the people of Israel
and the land of Israel must be present to insure the healing of both.
Indeed, no other people group or nation on earth was ever promised
a national spiritual restoration that is intimately related and
dependent upon their return to their ancient homeland!

Surely, the season of shame has ended. Both people and land
are being cleansed of their uncleanness, healed of their wounds, and
restored. Yet, their restoration to God's order, blessing and ultimate
glory is pending upon and directly related to their full and complete
restoration one to another!

18

Dirty Footprints in the Holy Place

A Lesson in History

In order to understand and appreciate the magnitude of the miraculous regathering of the people of Israel to their land, and the intensity of hateful resistance from the enemy's camp, it would be helpful to briefly review the historical background of the region.

When my grandparents pioneered their way into the Promised Land in the early years of this century, the territory was named "Palestine." The actual origin of the term "Palestine" can be traced to the Roman Emperor Hadrian who changed the name of the land from "Judea" to "Syria Palestina" after the final Roman victory in A.D. 135. At that time, many of the Jewish inhabitants were exiled, their property confiscated, and the territory renamed and designated to the Roman district of Syria. Jerusalem itself was razed and rebuilt as a Roman city named "Aelia Capitolina."

All these steps were taken in a deliberate attempt to obscure the truth, distort the facts of biblical history, and thus erase the Jewish territorial claim, cutting off their roots from the land of Israel. This diabolic plan, carried out through Roman policy to void the Word of God, was not successful. In fact, throughout all future centuries of foreign domination there remained a Jewish presence in the land that often constituted the majority of its few inhabitants.

Foreign powers dominated the land of Israel in succession for centuries. After Judea was destroyed by the Romans and her name changed, the Roman rule continued until the breakup of their empire and the rise of the Byzantine Empire in A.D. 315. The region was then ruled by the Byzantines until the advent of Islam and the capture of the land in A.D. 637. From this point to A.D. 1072, the land was ruled by various Moslem caliphs whose capitals were established in other lands. The land of Israel, or Palestine as it was called, was thus ruled for centuries from Arabia, Syria, Iraq, and then Egypt.

The Seljukes ruled for a brief period, then the land fell to the Crusaders in A.D. 1099, and was under their general rule until A.D. 1291. From this point until A.D. 1516 the land was dominated by the Mameluks from Egypt. At that time, the Ottoman Turkish Empire took over and controlled the whole region until the Turks were removed by the British in 1918. The area was then under the Mandate of Britain, who was commissioned by the League of Nations (the predecessor of the United Nations) to reconstruct the entire region and prepare a national home for the Jewish people in Palestine according to the 1917 Balfour Declaration. After much debate, struggle, and the horror of the holocaust, Israel was declared a sovereign state on May 14, 1948.

Indeed, empires and kingdoms had their season. Mighty armies rocked the whole region under their campaigns, yet they are all gone. Truly, **Jerusalem is the city where empires are buried!** Zechariah, as he unfolds the prophetic scenario of God's great deliverance of Israel at the end of the age, said, **"In that day I will make the clans of Judah like a firepot among pieces of wood and a flaming torch among sheaves, so they will consume on the right hand and on the left all the surrounding peoples, while the inhabitants of Jerusalem again dwell on their own sights in Jerusalem"** (Zech 12:6). This last phrase actually reads in the original Hebrew text that **Jerusalem shall dwell where Jerusalem always was.**

None of these rulers had much regard for the ancient homeland of the Jewish people. As foreign armies marched back and forth throughout the land, abusing and expelling its inhabitants, the soil itself was left uncultivated, wells were plugged up, salt was actually spread on the fields to ruin future fruitfulness, and forests were mowed down systematically. The whole of the ecological system was severely damaged, rainfall greatly diminished, topsoil became dust to be blown away, and life-giving rivers turned into malaria-infested swamps.

In fact, none of the conquering powers invested in the land or established any of their governing capitals there. The land called Palestine was, for thousands of years, no more than a backwater district for transient heathen empires. Truly, the words of Ezekiel took on an awesome and terrible meaning throughout history as he prophesied to the land of Israel, **"Thus says the Lord God, 'For good cause they [the nations] have made you desolate and crushed you from every side, that you should become a possession of the rest of the nations, and you have been taken up in the talk and the whispering of the people' "** (Ezekiel 36:3).

The Palestinian Issue

Nearly nineteen hundred years have elapsed since Israel entered the season of judgment and shame; these were years of desolation and despair for both people and land, separated one from another and from God. And, as we progressively enter the season of restoration, we find that the healing move of God is again resisted by spiritual powers and principalities and challenged by hostile governments and movements. Israel's ancient enemies have resurfaced simultaneously with her in our century, and illegal claims and pressures are again made toward the land.

The Arab nations surrounding Israel are, in fact, relatively new nations carved out from the conquered Ottoman Empire by the British and French after World War I. As these nations are still under the influence of the Islamic spirit, they find it religiously intolerable to co-exist as equals (without being dominant) with a people of a different faith living in the same region. Thus, as we will describe in detail in chapter nineteen, the Arab nations' ongoing conflict with Israel is fueled by nothing less than demonically induced religious aggression.

In the context of the overall Arab panorama, however, we will specifically address the Palestinian claim to both national and territorial integrity. This claim, which is in direct confrontation with the very existence and survival of Israel, has become so accepted and popular in recent years that the average person rarely questions the reality and truthfulness behind it. Was there ever an Arab country called "Palestine"? Was there ever a "Palestinian people" who formed and enjoyed a recognizable national life?

The spokesmen of the Palestinian "national movement," and specifically the leadership of the Palestine Liberation Organization (PLO), realized that if a lie is told loudly enough and often enough it eventually is perceived as truth. The fact is that the myth of the historic Palestinian state, so cleverly constructed over the years, has gained global authenticity, fooling even those who should know better. This mythical state has already been accepted and given observer status in the United Nations; Yasser Arafat has been named its president and, in several nations around the world, this mythical state has ambassadorial status!

The real tragedy, of course, has to do with the real people who live and raise their children behind the political propaganda and the media headlines. Indeed, while the Palestinian population is mostly made up of innocent families and clans caught in the power struggle of the Middle East, they are, nevertheless, kept in ignorance, manipulated and misguided by evil men.

During the entire period of recorded history, the land called "Palestine" was never ruled by "Palestinians." The fact is that, apart from the continuing Jewish presence in the land from A.D. 135 to 1948, its inhabitants consisted of the soldiers of each conquering army and their slaves.

Century after century, the culture, social fabric and identity of these inhabitants changed as the rulers changed. The Jews, on the other hand, are the sole survivors of the ancient population of the land. They alone have maintained an uninterrupted link with the land since the dawn of recorded history.

Who Are The Palestinians?

Prior to 1948, the term "Palestine" carried only regional significance without any national connotation, and likewise, the term "Palestinian" carried no national status whatsoever. There was never a Palestinian government, language, anthem or any defined national traditions. In fact, all of the people living in the region were called Palestinians.

Ironically, this identity was mostly used for the Jewish residents of the region during the British Mandate, and the national newspaper, now named "The Jerusalem Post," was actually called "The Palestine Post." After 1948, the Jewish residents of the new state of Israel took on the name "Israelis," while the Arab inhabitants assumed sole rights to the term "Palestinian," thus developing an identity apart from other Arab nationalities in the region.

Today the Palestinian Arabs are divided into three groups: First are the Israeli Arabs who were living in Israeli territory during the formation of the state. They comprise nearly twenty percent of the population of Israel and are citizens with full rights in this democratic country. These Arabs carry Israeli passports, have access to every Israeli institution, and have equal privileges and responsibilities with the Israeli Jews in areas such as voting, holding public offices, and serving in the parliament.

The second group are those living in Judea, Samaria and the Gaza strip, territories which were claimed in battle during the Six-Day War of 1967. Most live in their own villages and homes, while some live in refugee camps set up by the Jordanians and the U.N. in 1948. Those camps were established to absorb the Arab population which left the State of Israel at the time of the War of Independence in 1948. Responding to promises from the leaders of the invading Arab armies, these families withdrew from the Jewish communities in anticipation of a swift Arab victory and their own return to capture and possess Jewish property.

However, Israel gained the upper hand during this desperate war initiated by her neighbors, and the fleeing Arab families never returned to their homes. It is of significance to remember that the leaders of the Jewish community, at the time, pled with the departing Arabs to stay with their homes and businesses in preparation for a peaceful, democratic rule. Tragically, thousands of families were carried by the flood of deception, only to get trapped in refugee camps.

The third group of Palestinian Arabs consists of those who emigrated completely outside the area into neighboring Arab countries and other nations around the world. Depending on their hosting nation, these families found shelter and livelihood, sometimes exceeding those of their relatives left in the Middle East.

The ancestors of the majority of these Palestinian Arabs arrived in "Palestine" only within the past 100 to 200 years. It is well documented that Arab masses flooded into Palestine from all over the decaying Ottoman Empire, seeking jobs provided by Jewish commercial and developmental activities which began in the late 1800s. The myth of an indigenous Palestinian Arab population, that which goes back for generations, is a fallacy and a blatant lie. And while there are certain families and clans who can prove their roots in the land, they represent only a small fraction of the whole of the Arab Palestinian population of today.

Palestine was never an established Arab nation wrestled away forcefully by the Zionists, as is so often proclaimed by Arab propagandists. Rather, the Arab families who came for work felt no political ties to the land and, until the 1920s, no national community at all had even existed in Palestine. This is the reason why both the Balfour Declaration of England in 1917 and the League of Nations Mandate following World War I charged the Jewish population in Palestine with guaranteeing the civil and religious rights of minorities in the land. No mention was made, whatsoever, of any distinct "national" rights of these minorities, as it was clearly recognized by all parties that the only national claim to the area was that of the Jewish population.

It is interesting to note that, in all the years of Moslem domination, Palestine, and especially Jerusalem, was never the focus of any national aspirations. Palestine was always an undeveloped, neglected and insignificant province of the Moslem empires. Jerusalem itself was never a Moslem capital or even a cultural center, although a Moslem holy place was established on the site of the ancient Jewish temple. This practice of appropriating Jewish landmarks and cities for themselves has continued through the centuries, and archaeologists have discovered that names of hundreds of seemingly Arab villages were, in fact, Arab renderings of ancient biblical Hebrew names.

Undoubtedly, no hallmarks of any national identity could be found in Palestine until the establishment of the state of Israel. The land itself, as described earlier, was sorely neglected and undeveloped. In fact, the Arabs themselves, in the first quarter of the century, recognized the land as being a home for the Jews and expressed, in general, a very cordial acceptance.

This was clearly demonstrated in an agreement between Emir Feisal of Arabia and Dr. Chaim Weizmann of the World Zionist Organization. The Emir, a recognized spokesman for the Arabs at the time, spoke with much favor of the future cooperation between the Arabs and the Jews in founding their states. In Article 1 the Emir said, "The Arab state and Palestine (the Jewish state), in all their relations and undertakings, shall be controlled by the most cordial good will and understanding." The Emir clearly identified and welcomed the emergence of a Jewish nation in Palestine, parallel to the emergence of Arab nations in Arabia and the rest of the region under the British and French mandates.

In his letter to Felix Frankfurter, a U.S. Supreme Court justice, in 1919, the Emir further wrote, "We feel that the Arabs and Jews are cousins in race, having suffered similar oppression . . . and by happy coincidence have been able to take the first step toward the attainment of their national ideals together. The Arabs . . . look with deepest sympathy on the Zionist movement . . . We will wish the Jews a hearty welcome home."

All this accord and generosity changed dramatically in the coming years as the British pursued their own selfish goals in the Middle East. The fact is that the collapsing British empire created the myth of "Palestinian nationalism" for their own political and economic purposes. Britain actually succumbed to Arab pressures and political manipulation as their need for Arabian oil increased and World War II loomed on the horizon.

Land for (False) Peace

While the phrase "land for peace" has become a household word in terms of Middle Eastern dynamics, it is not a new expression but rather carries quite a historic cargo. Britain made two sets of territorial promises under her Mandate—one to the Moslems and the other to the Jews. These official promises were originally fully reconcilable and attainable.

The interesting historical fact is that between World War I and the U. N. partition of "Palestine" in 1947, British promises to the Arabs in the region were generously fulfilled, while their promises to the Jewish population were constantly violated. The Arabs were favored, as nearly twenty sovereign states were artificially carved out and established by the British from the former Turkish Empire. In actuality, these new nations, such as Syria, Iraq, Jordan and Kuwait, had no previous national history or separate cultures whatsoever.

However, the development of the part of "Palestine" allocated by the major powers to the Jews took a different course. The first "land for peace" agreement took place when four-fifths of the promised Jewish homeland was given to the Hashamite family, an Arabian royal line imported from Saudi Arabia by the British. They were established as the ruling family in the present kingdom of Jordan in 1946, and were handed seventy-eight percent of the original land promised to the Jewish people as a homeland by the League of Nations. In fact, the state of Israel today exists on the remaining one-fifth of the land originally promised. Yet, this loss of land provided no peace.

During the 1930s, as Hitler was rising into power in Germany, nearly 100,000 German Jewish refugees found shelter in Palestine. This caused great agitation among the Arab leadership, accompanied by murderous campaigns during which whole Jewish communities in Palestine were terrorized and slaughtered for three consecutive years. The British, anxious to draw the Arabs away from Nazi Germany, issued the notorious "McDonald White Paper" of 1939 which put an absolute stop to the Jewish immigration. Europe was ready to snare and destroy its Jewish population, and there was nowhere for them to go.

Worse yet, the British promised the Arabs, contrary to the previous international agreements, that in ten years "Western Palestine," (present day Israel), would become a sovereign Arab state. Jews, of course, would be permitted to live in it, but only as long as they did not amount to more than one-third of the total population. Indeed, the original mandate entrusted to England by the League of Nations was thus completely violated!

As millions of Jews were trapped in Europe, the leaders of the Jewish community in Israel demanded the end of the British Mandate. The Arabs, on the other hand, demanded that all of Palestine should become one nation with an Arab majority. And as the matter was debated and decided in the newly formed United Nations, the vote was cast for a sovereign Jewish state to be established.

However, there were serious problems with this U.N. plan, as this small territory, comprising only twenty-two percent of the original promised area, was further partitioned into two states, Palestinian and Jewish. This newly formed Jewish state was, in fact, made up of three disconnected regions, most of which were desert. Judea, Samaria, Gaza, and much of the Galilee were lost, while Jerusalem was to become an international city within the Palestinian state. Yet, after much agonizing debate, the leadership of the Jewish population accepted the plan, and on May 14, 1948, the new state was declared sovereign and was named Israel. However, this sacrifice of land did not produce the desired peace either!

The Arabs rejected the U.N. partition plan, as they wanted all of the land! On May 15, the armies of Lebanon, Jordan, Syria, Egypt and Iraq invaded the one-day-old state of Israel as the Mufti (an Arab religious leader) of Jerusalem proclaimed, **"I declare a holy war, my Moslem brothers! Murder the Jews! Murder them all!"**

Ironically, these five neighboring Arab states, totalling an area of 1,200,000 square miles, attempted to swallow up that tiny nation consisting of 8000 square miles! Yet, after almost a year of fierce fighting, the small Jewish community in Israel, fighting at odds of nearly 1 to 1000, won back parts of Galilee, Judea, Samaria, and liberated half of Jerusalem. In fact, many of the fighting soldiers were fresh arrivals from the European concentration and death camps with hardly any training and no command of Hebrew. Indeed, the victory of this untrained and poorly equipped army was nothing short of a miracle.

However, as the Arab armies retreated and agreed to an armistice, Jordan annexed the rest of Judea, Samaria and east Jerusalem as its own. This illegal act was never recognized by the

U.N., and these territories soon became breeding grounds from which to launch terrorist attacks against Israel's civilian population. Ironically, Jordan and Egypt were now occupying the West Bank and the Gaza strip, the very territories allotted to the Arab Palestinians under the U.N. Partition Plan of 1947, which they themselves earlier rejected. Thus, the Arab inhabitants of these territories were virtually taken over by their own Moslem brethren and kept as subjugated people from that point on.

Unfortunately, the "land for peace" formula never worked. It appears that the spirit which is behind the territorial lust of Arab expansionism is not at all interested in land, but in the total annihilation of the Jewish state. Thus, it will never be satisfied with partial settlements!

The fact is that God, in His love for the Arab people, granted them great tracts of land. The territory of the sons of Ishmael is 672 times the size of the state of Israel. It is twice the size of the United States as it embraces all of Northern Africa and the Arabian peninsula, and has treasures of oil. Still, the driving spirit behind the blinded masses continues to push for and pursue the destruction of Israel. Land is not its goal, and peace is not an option!

The Palestinian Tragedy

Cruelly and against basic human compassions, the Arab residents of Judea, Samaria and the Gaza strip were kept as refugees by their own brethren following the 1948 defeat. For the purpose of political manipulation, the neighboring Arab states kept these Arab Palestinians underprivileged and unable to improve their conditions.

These poor refugees fled Israel, never to return to loot and to spoil the abandoned Jewish communities as their leaders had promised. They now were locked in a prison of dirty politics, blackmail and abuse. They were given no economic opportunities, little education, and no industrial infrastructure whatsoever! They had become a political card in the hands of evil men trying to deceive the world and pressure Israel into compromises.

Why were they kept in such impoverished conditions until 1967 when Israel recaptured those territories? Why were they not allowed to blend into the Arab societies surrounding them with which they were comfortable and familiar? Why did Jordan never establish an independent Palestinian state in the West Bank during the nineteen years she ruled the territory?

All these and more are questions which must be answered. The tragedy and suffering of the Palestinian people could have been easily averted if handled properly by Arab leaders at the time. In fact, this could have been the simplest refugee problem of our century, given the fact that these refugees could have been easily absorbed into neighboring populations of like culture, religion, language and traditions.

We deal, however, not with human reasoning but with demonic powers and principalities who oppose God and His plan in the region. The chronic nature of the Palestinian cry, the intensifying pressure and stress it creates, and the deep deception surrounding it, all testify to the demonic origin of this tragedy. As Christians, we must maintain a heart of compassion and an attitude of intercession toward these abused and suffering people.

The fact is that land will never buy peace in the Middle East. Despite its recent public acceptance of Israel's right to exist, a statement made solely for the sake of Western politicians, the PLO's recorded covenant and stated goal is still the annihilation of the state of Israel. According to the PLO's "Phased Program," adopted at the Palestinian National Counsel in 1974 and reconfirmed in 1988, the PLO will act in phases to realize its strategic goal which is "the liberation of all of Palestine"!

Unable to defeat Israel by sudden attack at present, the ongoing deceptive plan is to act gradually; first, it aims to seize control of the West Bank and the Gaza strip by establishing a sovereign Palestinian state governed by the PLO, and then to force Israel back to the disadvantaged borders of the 1947 U.N. Partition Plan. In such a case, as Israel shrinks and her borders are hardly defensible, the enemy hopes that they will then collapse under an all-Arab attack, and Israel would finally be eliminated altogether from Middle Eastern soil. This initial step of setting up a Palestinian state in the West Bank and Gaza is but a staging post for a phased plan to annihilate Israel—to finish off her Jewish population and to dominate the land.

Meanwhile, more than one million Palestinian Arabs are trapped in this demonic political scheme, serving as pawns in this evil game.

And yet, we find comfort in the Word of God which not only establishes and protects the position of the alien in His land, but also promises a future harmony between the conflicting peoples.

Land for (True) Peace

As we know, this tiny piece of territory, comprising the only spot upon the face of the earth promised biblically to the Jewish nation as a home and a shelter, has been at the pinnacle of international attention for the last fifty years. One-third of all U.N. resolutions since 1948 were directly made either against or in regard to Israel. Why such a disproportionate amount of attention? Why such a thorn in the side of a predominately godless world?

Is it possible that Isaiah's ancient prophecy is being fulfilled before our very eyes? Is it not the promised **"standard for the nations"** (Is 11:12) that God is raising before an evil and unbelieving generation, attempting to draw all flesh to His truth and sovereignty? Could it be that Satan understands God's plan and is throwing into battle everything he has in order to manipulate and distort the turn of events? Indeed, it is!

Because of the centrality of Israel's return to her land in God's overall plan of redemption, all hell resists her. Since a redeemed Israel is a key component in God's last days strategy, and since Israel's redemption is intimately linked to her possession of the land (see Ez 36), that land is now targeted by high-ranking demonic principalities. If the people could only be destroyed, as the Nazis attempted in the holocaust, or if the land could only be denied them, as in the Palestinian conspiracy, then God's plan could be averted.

Yet, we know that God will triumph! His Word is established in the heavenlies from everlasting to everlasting and **must** be fulfilled. Nevertheless, there is ample room in the plan of God for faith, obedience and sacrifice to arise from a loving and believing church who has learned to intercede according to God's purposes. These prayers and petitions are the very spiritual muscle which can empower and assure the fulfillment of the prophetic Word.

There is "land for peace" in the Middle East. God, in His kindness and faithfulness, has decreed the land of Israel to return to the sole possession of the people of Israel. After 1,900 years the land again is prospering. After 1,900 years the people again are settling under their own fig trees and vines. And, as imperfect and challenged as this scenario is, it nevertheless points to and reaches toward the perfect fulfillment of all scriptural prophecy.

Israel will turn back to God. He will purge and purify this nation for Himself, and then vindicate His Holy Name in their midst before the eyes of an amazed and bewildered world (Ez 36:23-24). This troubled land will yield peace—eternal and enduring peace—for all who believe in His Name.

19

Esau and Jacob Reconciled!

As we look into the conflicts and the many challenges still ahead of us in the Middle East, we lift up our eyes to one of the highest and most noble revelations God has provided. Not only must we believe that in the cross of Jesus the dividing wall between Jew and Gentile (including Arabs) was broken down, and that there is a future promise for peace and harmony in the region according to Isaiah 19:23-25, but we also find a prophetic picture of Jewish-Arab reconciliation in the story of Esau and Jacob. This revelation is widely shared among intercessors these days, and is a significant biblical endorsement for the reconciliation move between believers in these two groups.

In Genesis, chapters 32 and 33, we find the account of Jacob's return to his father's homeland after years of exile. The nature and dynamics of this occasion serve as a prophetic correlation, providing insight and inspiration for intercession, as we compare it to the return of the Jewish people to their land in our days. Esau represents the Arab people who are in the region. Jacob stands for the Jewish population returning after years of exile.

The Trauma

Undoubtedly, there was much excitement and anticipation in Jacob's heart as he neared the land of his fathers. His roots were already pulled out from the heathen soil of Laban's questionable hospitality, and his camp was moving westward with wives, children and possessions. Yet, there was also a deep concern within his soul as he girded himself to face his own dubious past, his relatives and, especially, his offended brother, Esau.

Jacob's prayer, **"Deliver me, I pray, from the hand of my brother, from the hand of Esau; for I fear him, lest he come and attack me, the mothers with the children"** (Gen 32:11), gives us insight into the struggle of his soul. Yes, there is excitement in his heart! Yes, there are hopeful expectations in the hearts of the returning Jews! But there is also great fear and concern for Arab retaliation.

Whether or not Esau was planning to harm Jacob is unclear, yet Jacob's fears were very real, moving him to take definite actions. Likewise, while it may seem unbelievable to the Arab nations, Israel's military and foreign policy are primarily motivated by her concern for survival. It is the urgent need to secure her physical existence that dominates Israel's political and strategic considerations.

How I wish that the Arab mind would comprehend this trauma! How I hope for the world to understand Israel's recoil and reaction to centuries of prolonged animosity and hatred from the descendants of Esau! Indeed, the scripture is true in describing God's anger toward the Arab hostilities, saying, " **'Because you have had everlasting enmity and have delivered the sons of Israel to the power of the sword at the time of their calamity, at the time of the punishment of the end, therefore, as I live,' declares the Lord God, 'I will give you over to bloodshed, and bloodshed will pursue you; since you have not hated bloodshed, therefore bloodshed will pursue you' "** (Ez 35:5-6).

Crying Out to God

The mounting pressures which never seemed to subside, but only to increase, drove Jacob to God. After dividing his family and possessions into two camps, he cried out in prayer, **"O God of my father Abraham and God of my father Isaac, O Lord, who didst say to me, 'Return to your country and to your relatives, and I will prosper you,' I am unworthy of all the lovingkindness and of all the faithfulness which Thou hast shown to Thy servant"** (Gen 32:9-10). How refreshing it is to find genuine humility and gratitude in the heart of this man. And, not only was it clear to Jacob that God called him to return to the land, but also that the conflict with Esau drove him closer to the Lord.

Could it be that our present difficulty with the Palestinian Arabs will serve in driving the Jewish people back to God? Certainly, it was God's idea to restore the Jewish people to the land; God knew of the Arab presence in the region and of the future conflicts. Thus, we may conclude that not only is it God's will for the Jewish people to live in the land of their fathers and to be reconciled to the Arabs who are in the land, but that the conflict over that reconciliation will serve in bringing them back to Himself.

There will always be Arabs who do not want to see the Jews return to their land, just as there will always be Jews who do not want to be reconciled with Arabs. Still, God's Word clearly spells out the mandate for Jewish habitation in the land of Israel, as well as commanding us, in New Testament writings, toward personal and racial reconciliation.

In fact, according to this biblical model, one can say that Jacob could never be fully restored to the land of his fathers without first being reconciled to his brother, Esau! It is as if the challenge of reconciliation with the Arabs (to the extent that it is possible at any given time), is almost a prerequisite in order for the Jewish people to come into the fulness of their destiny. And though it may be naturally impossible in the foreseeable future, God looks into the hearts of men to see if they are willing to do His will. True reconciliation always requires deep humility and great courage born of faith in the Living God and in His purposes.

The Lord Jesus Himself taught us that we must first deal with the issue of reconciliation to a brother before we can be properly related to God in spiritual worship (Matt 5:23-24).

Encounter with God

The impossibility of appeasing Esau was as frustrating and crushing to Jacob as the impossibility of appeasing the Arabs is to the Jewish people today. Jacob sent gifts and then divided his camp into two groups in an attempt to protect his possessions, yet nothing seemed to help. Similarly, there are no human solutions to the present conflict in the Middle East. Whether self-defense, political maneuvering or land concessions, none will provide the answer.

In fact, when Jacob prayed, **"I will appease him with the present that goes before me"** (Gen 32:20), he made use of the Hebrew root, "KAPAR," which is the word used for atonement. He was actually attempting to make atonement before his brother for his sin. But there is no atonement without divine intervention.

At last Jacob was left with only his own soul and the reality of God to reckon with. He had done all he could, and he used every human manipulation possible. Now he must face himself and his God!

As he separated himself and was alone, he immediately was confronted with the messenger of God, with whom he wrestled all through the night (v 24). This night was not only to determine the outcome of his immediate conflict with Esau, but was to become a turning point in Jacob's destiny and in his relationship with God.

The divine messenger, who is called both God and man, had Jacob disclose his identity. This was, of course, a type of confession, as the name **Jacob** means "Heel Grabber" and described his carnal and manipulative character. And upon this profession, the messenger changed Jacob's name to Israel, which means "One Who Wrestles with God" and, also, "One Who is a Prince with God."

Thus, as the mounting pressures impelled Jacob to face the God of his fathers, deal with his own carnal nature, and consider his destiny, so it will be with the Jewish people in the last days. While in the clutches of a seemingly unresolvable conflict with the Arab relatives, they, too, will wrestle with a mysterious God-man messenger in the darkness of their night. They, too, will confess their sin and carnal nature, and they, too, will be raised with renewed vitality and identity at the dawn of a new day.

Indeed, if we recognize the prophetic integrity of this biblical picture, we must realize that the Jewish-Arab conflict and the struggle for reconciliation will lead to the transformation and the spiritual reviving of the children of Israel. Truly, we may not see the fulness of the promised revival sweep throughout Israel until the nation properly faces the spiritual dynamics surrounding this issue and, in desperation, casts herself upon the Lord.

Reconciled!

Coming out of the transforming presence of the Living God, **"Now the sun rose upon [Jacob] just as he crossed over Penuel, and he was limping on his thigh"** (Gen 32:31). Indeed, a new day, and a new man! Jacob was now ready to face Esau. Unafraid and full of grace, he bows down to the ground seven times before his former foe. Oh, how wonderful to be so at rest with himself and with God that he can humble himself and honor his older brother, Esau. And anyone who is familiar with the Arab culture will appreciate the significance of showing respect and honor as the balm to heal many wounds and offenses.

And what was Esau's response? What is the only response when one faces the fulness of grace, humility and confidence that is in the anointing of God? The scripture says that Esau **"ran to meet him and embraced him, and fell on his neck and kissed him, and they wept"** (Gen 33:4).

Surely, buried deep in the heart of the Jews and the Arabs is a desire to be reconciled and to put an end to war. Behind all the political rhetoric, the historic offenses, and the demonic manipulation of hostile carnal minds, there is that hope for true peace. And, when the time arrives, when modern "Jacob" has wrestled with the God of his fathers and is humbled and resurrected while facing his Messiah, both peoples will embrace one another and fall upon one another's necks with tears of joy.

For indeed, so profound is that moment that Jacob said to his brother, **"for I see your face as one sees the face of God"** (Gen 33:10). Somehow, for Jacob the healing of that ancient family wound was a reminder of his encounter with the God-man the night before.

The loving face of Esau reminded him of the face of God! And, indeed, so profound will be the true reconciliation between Arab and Jew that it will help us all to see God's face.

20

Islam—The Spiritual Battle

Concerning God's judgments, the Bible says, **"And His voice shook the earth then, but now He has promised, saying, 'Yet once more I will shake not only the earth, but also the heaven.' And this expression, 'Yet once more,' denotes the removing of those things which can be shaken, as of created things, in order that those things which cannot be shaken may remain"** (Heb 12:26-27).

The Great Shaking

One of the many glorious promises reserved for the last days is that of a great shaking. This promised shaking has obviously begun and is testing the very foundations of our societies and cultures. Even as we write these words, every ideological, social, political and economic structure is being shaken and tried to the core throughout the world. And as national movements are rising, violently struggling to define themselves after centuries of oppression, we find the human race asking questions it cannot answer.

Yet, these supernatural tremors which constitute part of the great end-time birth pains are not limited to the earthly or physical creation alone. Rather, the scriptural promise is for these shakings to extend to the heavens as well. "Yet once more I will shake not only the earth, but also the heaven." Indeed, not only are human governments and earthly systems experiencing God's testing, but so are "rulers . . . powers . . . world forces of this darkness [and] spiritual forces of wickedness," whose activity in the spirit realm prevails upon and exploits the masses of undiscerning humanity (Eph 6:12).

The voice of the Lord is already thundering in the heavenlies. He is marshalling His armies for the final confrontations of the age, shaking and dismantling the strongholds of hell. Communism, for example, is a major principality and world power that God has brought down with His swift judgment, liberating millions of souls from its oppression. In nation after nation, this ungodly, antichrist conspiracy is losing its terrorizing grip, as entire societies enter into freedom.

Isaiah speaks of this unprecedented time. He writes, "The earth is shaken violently. The earth reels to and fro like a drunkard, and it totters like a shack, for its transgression is heavy upon it . . . So it will happen in that day, that the Lord will punish the host of heaven ["the fallen angels in the heavens," LB], on high, and the kings of the earth, on earth" (Is 24:19-21).

Indeed, the world is filling up the cup of its transgressions, and God's righteous judgments increasingly manifest as large-scale calamities and global traumas accumulate. However, according to this scripture, His judgments first take place in the heavenly realm, and only then do they manifest on earth. Truly, there is an undeniable link between the spiritual influence of the fallen "host of heaven" and the conditions and outcome of the "kings of the earth."

The psalmist offers us another perspective of this shaking: "When Israel went forth from Egypt . . . The mountains skipped like rams, the hills, like lambs . . . Tremble, O earth, before the Lord, before the God of Jacob" (Ps 114:1,4,7). As God delivered His people from their bondage, creation itself trembled at the issue of

His judgments and deliverance. The Lord Himself went before His people as the **"Lord of Hosts,"** the Captain of the armies of the Most High God, and the earth trembled before Him! Indeed, not only were the "gods" of Egypt cast down through Moses' spiritual warfare, bringing down with them the mightiest empire of those days, but the natural dimensions themselves responded to the moving of the Lord.

In the context of the unleashing of Christ's redeeming power over the nations of the world and over Israel today, He is warring to end the captivity of His people. And again, creation itself is shaking as He extracts His harvest and judges His enemies.

We who are in Christ are truly privileged to be a part of this generation. Yet, with privilege comes responsibility as God calls us to participate in His plan and cooperate with His will. For, concerning the godly ones the psalmist testifies, **"Let the high praises of God be in their mouth, and a two-edged sword in their hand, to execute vengeance on the nations, and punishment on the peoples; to bind their kings with chains, and their nobles with fetters of iron; to execute on them the judgment written; This is an honor for all His godly ones. Praise the Lord!"** (Ps 149:6-9) Indeed, it is our honor and reward to be a part of the execution of God's will.

We must understand the nature of the conflict in the Middle East. One of these "world rulers" whom the Lord is confronting— a principality with global authority and influence—is the spirit of Islam, which fiercely dominates the Middle East and seeks to infiltrate even to the West.

The Middle Eastern conflict is not merely political, economic or military, although all of these elements are certainly present. The primary battleground in this conflict is spiritual; its true origin is in the heavenlies and the outcome of it will be determined by our prayers and our anointed spiritual warfare!

What is Islam?

Islam is a world religion which surfaced in the seventh century A.D. in the city of Mecca in Arabia. Mohammed, its primary prophet and founder, acted upon "revelations" and "visions" received from "Allah" while hidden in a cave. "Allah" was, in fact, one of the hundreds of demigods worshipped by the scattered Arab tribes at the time. This demon commanded Mohammed to abolish the rest of the idols, and "Allah" was now the "great god" of the Arab people. Thus, a world religion was born which appeared to be monotheistic.

The Koran, Islam's holy book, was then compiled by Mohammed to exert ultimate authority in all matters of life and worship. Mohammed gave much recognition to biblical truths, drawing from both Old and New Testament writings, even to the point of recognizing God's covenants with Israel, both natural and spiritual.

However, the "prophet" taught that both groups, the Jewish and the Christian people, failed God. He taught that their apostasy moved God to abolish His covenants with them, and he declared that "Allah," in turn, raised the Arab people as the **last covenant people** by giving them the last revelation—the Moslem teachings!

The word **Islam** means "**submission**," which is the heart of this religion. Islam's utmost mission and expressed goal is to bring every person, and the world as a whole, into submission to "Allah" in accordance with the teachings of the Koran. The methods this spirit employs are "soul-winning" (presenting a super-religious and self-righteous facade) and the "Jihad" (territorial expansion through Holy War). Either way, they insist, the world must ultimately submit to "Allah"!

Incredible as this may be, Islam is the second largest religion in our world today and is growing fast. Nearly one billion souls are "submitted" today to the "great Allah," and the numbers are increasing. Yet, we have heard the Lord say, "No more!"

This principality, which has successfully penetrated into nearly every region of our globe and is ruling one-fifth of its population, is vehemently anti-Christ. A well-accepted teaching of Islam claims that the prophet spoken of in Deuteronomy 18:15-19 is none other than Mohammed! We know that Moses clearly prophesied in this passage concerning Jesus the Messiah in whose mouth God would put His Word. Yet, Islam teaches that Mohammed is that future fulfillment of Moses, and that in his mouth is found the word of God. Truly, Satan is a liar and a thief, seeking to pervert God's Word and deceive the ignorant.

Islam built its third most holy site, the Dome of the Rock, on Mount Moriah in Jerusalem, the very site of the ancient Hebrew temple. It teaches that on this site Abraham offered up Ishmael (not

Isaac), and that from this location Mohammed later ascended into heaven mounted on his white horse. This blatant twist of truth distorts the biblical accounts of both the offering of Isaac and the Lord's ascension into heaven after His resurrection!

Islam claims to believe in the historic Jesus, yet **vehemently denies His divinity, His substitutional death on the cross and His resurrection from the dead.** It teaches that the great "Allah" "whisked" Jesus, the prophet, from the cross before his death, taking him to heaven. Jesus, according to Islam, was a great teacher and prophet just like Moses, Mohammed and other spiritual leaders. Thus, the Moslem faith will never submit to the Lordship of Jesus as Messiah, Savior and Son of the Living God.

At the top of the Dome of the Rock on Mount Moriah in Jerusalem are found inscriptions in Arabic saying in effect, **"God is not begotten; neither does He beget. God has no son; He needed no son. Worship 'Allah' alone."** These particular statements, followed by many like them, are quoted from the Koran which the Moslems believe to be the uncreated, eternal word of God. How tragic it is that these inscriptions adorn this Moslem place of worship in Jerusalem, the very city of the Lord Jesus' crucifixion and resurrection.

As stated before, Moslems believe they have replaced both Jews and Christians as the present covenant people of God. Consequently, we can better appreciate the offense and hatred generated by the presence of Jewish Israel and "Christian" Lebanon in the Arab heartland, the Middle East. The countries of Israel and Lebanon are the two primary Middle Eastern nations where the gospel can be, and is, openly and legally preached; therefore, it is no wonder they both are engulfed in the flames of unrestrained demonic hatred and violence! Both Israel's and Lebanon's territorial and sovereign presence in the Middle East are intolerable for fundamental Islam, as their very existence threatens and defies Islam's ultimate goal of world domination. This, precisely, is where **"Jihad,"** the Holy War, comes into play.

The late Ayatollah Khomeini of Iran was quoted as saying: "Israel is Satan and the United States is the great Satan." This belief is widespread among many devoted Moslems. Interestingly, Khomeini ruled over Iran, which is not even an Arab nation in the classic sense of the word! This country used to be Persia, ruled by the liberal shah, yet fell headlong one generation ago into the jaws of fundamental Islam. Since then, nation after nation has been swallowed up by the unquenchable appetite of this violent lustful spirit. Today, almost the whole Arab world (which was not all Moslem) is engulfed in the demonic frenzy of the "Islamic revolution." Arab governments are actually bullied, often to the point of defeat, by Moslem fanatics seeking to make the Koran the law of the land.

Additionally, a "Moslem revival" has been sweeping throughout the rest of the world. The ignorant swallow its lies, while the church tolerates it, as we have failed to recognize the power of this principality! In the United States alone, there are nearly three million practicing Moslems, some of them openly aspiring and striving for leadership positions in the political system. Their stated goal, amazingly enough, is to **turn America toward submission to the "great Allah,"** filling up the spiritual void the church should fill. We do not believe this will occur; however, we must take seriously this fierce principality with its all-consuming intent and the violent devotion of some of its extremist leaders and followers.

This world power is the chief enemy of God's purposes in the Middle East today. Its fierce violence and intense hatred surpass many of the forces which opposed Israel in other times, and is openly demonstrated in the region's perpetual wars and conflicts. No political negotiations, territorial compromises or superpower interventions could ever satisfy the lust of this principality. The fact is that even if Israel would be taken out of the picture, the Arab world is still sharply divided and at enmity among its various nations and factions. **Competition, treachery, violence and poverty afflict the Arab masses continually, as this principality devours its own slaves.**

Unfortunately, these Moslem nations forbid and severely punish any attempt to spread the gospel of the Kingdom of God; thus the misery and ignorance go on and on. In fact, Israel and Lebanon are the only Middle Eastern nations where Arab Moslems can be, and are, legally and openly won to Christ. Ironically, various mission organizations are testing their methods and training their workers for Arab evangelism in Israel.

The Lord's Deliverance

It is possible that the volatile conditions in the Middle East today are for the purpose of flushing out and exposing the spirit of Islam. Indeed, it is part of God's plan to bring every world system to its knees, liberating its masses, as the consummation of the age draws near. In 1991, for the first time in recent history, the Western world was forced to confront the deception, treachery and violence resident in the spirit of Islam as displayed in the Gulf War. It seemed as if Israel's plight was somewhat better understood for a brief moment.

Some of the Arab leaders, such as Assad of Syria, Quadhafi of Libya, and the current Ayatollah in Iran, given to the full sway of this spirit and other accompanying demonic powers, are the main points of penetration and influence through which this principality rules. Resisting anything Christian or Jewish, they actually breed hatred toward the revelation of the true, loving and living God.

Yet, the Lord has purposed to bring a harvest from every tribe, nation and people on the earth, and we expect a multitude of souls to come from the Arab nations as well. For these souls to hear the gospel and respond with liberty of faith, the ruling principality must be overthrown. This will not be done by political maneuvers or economic sanctions. **The battle is primarily spiritual and will be fought and won in the heavenlies.**

Wars will yet be fought over the Middle Eastern plains, mountains and deserts, yet we know for certain that it will be the fervent intercession of God's people that will bring His mercy and triumph into the affairs of man. The victory of the praying church in the spiritual battlefields will secure both Israel's survival and the proclamation of the gospel to the Arab masses.

Indeed, the Lord, **"not wishing for any to perish but for all to come to repentance"** (2 Peter 3:9), will strengthen our hands in this battle. As prayers and petitions are coupled with God-sent teams of laborers into the harvest, this principality of Islam, a world ruler of wickedness, will come down!

Let none be disqualified because of a fearful, unbelieving heart. The Lord Jesus Himself has put His prayer and His flame in the bosom of the church. God's Word to His servants who stand in the gap is: **Watch and pray, pray and watch, then pray again!**

21

The Removing of the Veil

"Having therefore such a hope, we use great boldness in our speech, and are not as Moses, who used to put a veil over his face that the sons of Israel might not look intently at the end of what was fading away. But their minds were hardened; for until this very day at the reading of the old covenant the same veil remains unlifted, because it is removed in Christ . . . but whenever a man turns to the Lord, the veil is taken away" (2 Cor 3:12-16).

A unique veil blinds the people of Israel. This veil was sovereignly placed over their spiritual eyes for a divine purpose. However, the scriptural promise is clear and leaves no room for doubt—this veil will be removed!

The spiritual restoration of the people of Israel, the opening of their hearts to receive the revelation of the Living God and His mercies in Messiah, is directly linked to their turning to the Lord. Indeed, the Spirit cried out through Isaiah the prophet, saying, "Turn [or look] to Me, and be saved, all the ends of the earth; for

I am God, and there is no other" (Is 45:22). It is in Israel's turning to the Lord out of her genuine need that the blindness will be lifted.

Peter, as well, when addressing the crowd in the temple, challenged them to "repent therefore and return, that your sins may be wiped away" (Acts 3:19). It will be when Israel, as a nation, looks to God under the conviction of His Spirit, realizing the purpose, identity and majesty of the Messiah, that the veil will be finally removed!

The humanistic mind might argue: "How can God expect those who have no sight to look at Him? How can He require them to see? It's not fair! It's impossible!" Yet the scriptures are unwavering regarding God's command, "Hear, you deaf! And look, you blind, that you may see" (Is 42:18). Indeed, it is at the point of absolute obedience to God's Word, as Israel simply humbles herself before Him as both Savior and Lord, that the healing will come, even to a people blinded for millenniums!

It is the humble gaze of faith and dependency that opens the gate of one's soul to see the glory of the Messiah. The ancient veil will be removed. The unbelief, fear and shame will be gone, as faith, love and hope take their place in the soul of the nation. However, the church needs to recognize the various layers and dynamics of that ancient veil in order to powerfully pray and labor for its removal.

Sin!
The First Layer

The deepest and most ancient layer of this veil is that which is common to all man—that very condition of the human heart which opposes God's authority over one's own soul and denies the need for a savior. This fallen state is best portrayed in Lucifer's words when he said, "I will ascend . . . I will raise my throne . . . I will make myself like the Most High" (Is 14:13-14). That assertion of one's own self above all that is holy and divine is not only inexcusable, but it brings with it devastating consequences.

Therefore, we find the first layer blinding Israel from seeing and perceiving God's truth is the "original sin"! So original and so all-encompassing this sin condition is, that we find this tragic description in the scriptures: "They have all turned aside; together they have become corrupt; there is no one who does good, not even one" (Ps 14:3).

How lamentable it is that these heartrending words had to be recorded in the holy scriptures! Indeed, it is a sad witness of an uncaring, unbelieving and unwise humanity. And for this sin, into which we all have been born, there is only one remedy—the blood of Christ! Only the blood of God's eternal covenant can atone for and do away not only with the consequences of our sin but with its very power over our lives!

In order to see this layer of the veil peeled back, the gospel in its entirety and fulness must be preached. There is no other means of salvation! Paul declared, **"I am not ashamed of the gospel, for it is the power of God for salvation to everyone who believes, to the Jew first and also to the Greek"** (Rom 1:16). Peter, too, had no other message to the Jewish population of his day when he preached in Jerusalem, **"Therefore let all the house of Israel know for certain that God has made Him both Lord and Christ—this Jesus whom you crucified . . . 'Repent, and let each of you be baptized in the name of Jesus Christ for the forgiveness of your sins; and you shall receive the gift of the Holy Spirit' "** (Acts 2:36,38). Only the full recognition of our sinfulness and utter helplessness will drive us to gratefully accept the gift of righteousness in the Messiah. And only then can we receive the Holy Spirit and be born again from above. This is true for both Jew and Gentile alike!

Let us never shrink back from preaching the gospel to the Jewish people. Yes, it may be offensive to hearts that are biased and calloused by a painful history. It may be resisted, hated and blasphemed. Yet we must remember that only the truth sets people free!

Traditions of Men
The Second Layer

The second layer of the veil consists of the volumes of rabbinical teachings and traditions accumulated over many centuries, which have blinded Israel from understanding God's true purpose. This complex and sophisticated maze of ethics, customs and regulations, covering every facet of life, actually found its origin during the Babylonian exile. In Babylon, Jewish scholars began to develop and elaborate their concepts of Jewish life and tradition, attempting to compile and identify the very essence of Judaism, while failing to recognize the fallen condition of the nation, her shame and self-deception at the time!

While under God's judgment and purging, far away from their homeland, these sages and scholars developed a system of thought and philosophy that would replace the prophetic unction, God's present and living Word, in the life of the nation. Tragically, the very prophetic ministry that alone could turn the nation back to God was now substituted by teachings of men. This, possibly, is one of the reasons for the small numbers that responded to Ezra and Nehemiah's prophetic mandate to return from Babylon to the land and to God!

These rabbinic writings continued to expand and multiply for hundreds of years, providing the very foundation for the course and flavor of Judaism. Many of these writings are purely the product of creative and sophisticated humanistic reasoning, with little biblical substance. In fact, the words of the rabbis, in many instances, have grown weightier and more influential than the words of God Himself.

A good example of this phenomenon is the religious upheaval that surrounded the miraculous return of the Ethiopian Jewish community to Israel a few years ago. These newcomers actually practice a Judaism which predates the rabbinical writings and is much more Mosaic and scriptural in nature! Their faith and religious practices threatened the rabbinical authorities of our day and triggered a storm of insecurities, pride and manipulations. To this day the power struggle continues, as rabbis attempt to "subdue" and "conform" the Ethiopian Jews to the rabbinical culture and traditions.

It was because of this that Stephen, in his heartrending cry to the religious hierarchy of his day, called out, **"You men who are stiff-necked and uncircumcised in heart and ears are always resisting the Holy Spirit; . . . Which one of the prophets did your fathers not persecute? . . . you who received the law as ordained by angels, and yet did not keep it"** (Acts 7:51-53). We can only imagine the contrast between the holy anger surging through Stephen's heart and the terrorizing rage in the hearts of his persecutors. **"Now when they heard this, they were cut to the quick, and they began gnashing** their teeth at him . . . and covered their ears, and they rushed upon him with one impulse . . . they began stoning him" (Acts 7:54-58).

Indeed, this deceived and demonized mob is a typical and tragic picture of the way religious traditions and humanistic philosophies often react to the holy presence of Jesus in His disciples! And as we consider the dynamics just described, we cannot miss the horrific confrontation between light and darkness over that field outside ancient Jerusalem. This crowd, filled with demonic rage, was murdering a holy man and was fully convinced they were serving God! So real is that second layer of the veil!

And so real was this veil upon Saul of Tarsus, one of Rabbi Gamaliel's prize disciples and chief persecutor of the early church, that when Ananias laid his hands upon him in the city of Damascus after his blinding encounter with the Lord, **"Immediately there fell from his eyes something like scales, and he regained his sight, and he arose and was baptized . . . and immediately he began to proclaim Jesus in the synagogues, saying, 'He is the Son of God' "** (Acts 9:18-20).

Once this layer of dead traditions and humanistic teachings was supernaturally stripped from his eyes, Saul became a Paul, and the persecutor of the church became the ambassador of the gospel. What an amazing transformation!

We must, however, keep in mind that our struggle is not against flesh and blood, but is spiritual, as was the case with Paul. And though men yield themselves as channels and vessels for these deceptive and blinding antichrist teachings, it is the spiritual principle and the power that is working through them with which we wrestle!

The Lie of History
The Third Layer

The third layer of the veil, as did the second layer, pertains exclusively to the Jewish people, as it is made up of the sorrow, suffering, and deep rejection which has filled their cup for thousands of years. Historically, the nation of Israel absorbed into her collective soul milleniums of hatred, persecution, and repeated attempts of annihilation.

From nation to nation and from century to century, the Jewish people were driven by the hands of their persecutors —from Pharaoh to Amalek, from Balak to the Philistines and from Haman to Hitler. And tragically, some of the greatest atrocities and offenses in the last two thousand years were committed by "Christians" under "Christian" banners.

In time, a condition developed in the soul of the Jewish nation which built a debilitating barrier, hindering the acceptance of any positive and comforting messages from the nations of the world. Even the truth of salvation could not penetrate through this veil of pain and disillusionment accumulated over the Jewish soul throughout the centuries!

Sadly, in the collective memory of Israel, true messengers of the gospel come at the end of a long and horrible line of recollections. These memories stretch from the anti-Semitic popes to the Catholic Inquisition, the bloody Crusades, the persecution under Martin Luther, the widespread European waves of murderous "pogroms," and down to Hitler and our present-day "Saddams."

It was Christian Crusaders in A.D. 1099 who locked Jewish families inside the great synagogue in Jerusalem, set it on fire, then marched around it singing, "Christ, we adore thee." Martin Luther, the father of the Reformation, wrote in his book, *The Jews and their Lies*, "What then shall we Christians do with this damned, rejected race of Jews? Since they live among us, and we know about their lying and blasphemy and cursing, we cannot tolerate them if we do not wish to share their lies, curses and blasphemy . . . we must prayerfully and reverentially practice a merciful severity." No wonder Hitler was convinced he was doing God's will in attempting to annihilate the Jewish people as he quoted from Luther!

An excellent study of this historic Jewish trauma is found in the book entitled, *Our Hands Are Stained With Blood*, by Michael L. Brown, available from Messiah Biblical Institute Bookstore, P.O. Box 7163, Gaithersburg, MD 20890-7167.

Naturally speaking, can one really expect Israel to start trusting the nations now? Can Israel believe that the Christian messengers suddenly changed and now bear good news for the Jew? History has proven the opposite!

This stronghold of rejection has become demonically induced and has so infiltrated the mind and soul of Israel that the nation is, by now, conditioned to doubt, suspect and reject the intentions of others. This stronghold greatly paralyzes Israel's ability to open up her heart toward the Christian message, the Christian messenger, and toward Christ Himself. Too much scar tissue of too many painful and costly memories blind the nation's vision and perception from beholding the loving hand of God stretched out to her with compassion and healing.

This third deadly layer of the veil will only be removed by a true demonstration of sacrificial and unconditional divine love. The wounds of rejection and isolation are so deep within the soul of Israel that only God's love and acceptance borne by human vessels will bring the healing. Love alone will conquer hatred, and only full acceptance will overcome this deep rejection!

To Stand in the Gap

Indeed, this is the challenge that is before the church today. We need to demonstrate God's truth with so much love that, while it cuts to the quick with conviction, it heals the ancient wounds with compassion. Truly, nothing less than the Spirit of Christ Himself in and through His people will suffice for this task. It is love which is melting the veil!

"And behold, the veil of the temple was torn in two from top to bottom, and the earth shook; and the rocks were split" (Matt 27:51). As with that ancient veil in the temple, the veil that is presently over the Jewish eyes and hearts will also be torn from top to bottom!

This is a call for intercession! The removing of this veil will start in the heavenly places where the prayers of the church first prevail and, in turn, change the conditions on earth. All of God's promises toward us are **"yes"** in Christ Jesus, and through Him the praying church offers her **"amen"** in intercession, travailing to possess them all!

22

The Stronghold
of Rejection

Israel: Set Apart

Even as the nation of Israel is presently caught up in the awesome move of God's healing and restoration, an ancient cry still wells up from deep within her wounded soul. Considering her isolation and rejection, David's words give a painful and realistic expression to this national sorrow which echoes through the corridors of time. **"Turn to me and be gracious to me, for I am lonely and afflicted. The troubles of my heart are enlarged; bring me out of my distresses. Look upon my affliction and my trouble, and forgive all my sins. Look upon my enemies, for they are many; and they hate me with violent hatred"** (Ps 25:16-19). For so long this has been the traumatic and sorrowful confession of this nation.

Ever since her inception with Father Abraham nearly 4,500 years ago, these words were Israel's cry, as she endured loneliness, affliction, distress, and hatred from others. Truly, Israel often brought her troubles upon herself, thus incurring God's judgments. Nevertheless, one cannot ignore the divine sovereignty which chooses one nation, setting her apart from the rest—"setting her up," as it were, for perpetual loneliness, vulnerability and rejection. Why? And for what purpose? Was the divine plan so harsh that God's choosing and setting apart was to result in Israel's global and continual rejection?

Again, in the context of instructing the sons of Israel to possess the land promised to them, and to uproot the ungodly pagan nations, the Lord declares: "**Hence I have said to you, 'You are to possess their land'... I am the Lord your God, who has separated you from the peoples... and I have SET YOU APART from the peoples to be Mine"** (Lev 20:24,26, emphasis mine). Indeed, the nation was set apart from the rest, divinely called and chosen to demonstrate and to manifest God's rule while expressing His goodness, holiness, and glory to a fallen world.

Separation Breeds Rejection

Together with the privileges and honor of being God's chosen nation, set apart for His purposes, Israel tasted of the bitter cup of opposition and rejection. It seems that the emerging presence of a liberated, worshipping people so provoked the demonic realm and threatened Satan's rule that he, in turn, stirred up trouble again and again to discourage and to enslave these people afresh!

As we study Israel's history, we cannot but recognize the presence of a deep national stronghold thousands of years old, which to this day shapes and manipulates Israel's perception of herself, of other nations, and of her God; **it is a stronghold of rejection.**

Consider Father Abraham: From the very conception of the nation, there was an unavoidable and undeniable sense of being a stranger. Never fully welcomed nor integrated, but merely tolerated by his contemporaries, Abraham wandered across the promised land, fending for himself and his clan again and again. It appears that because these people were **elected** by God for His purposes, they were **rejected** by the world. Indeed, that which God approves of and delights in is a scorn and a disdain in the eyes of the world.

Then came Isaac, the second generation of the covenant people, who was a natural fulfillment of the promised seed. In him were the promise and the destiny embodied. What a tremendous call he carried! And yet, where did it lead him but to the altar upon which he was bound and to the knife raised high over his chest. Surely, Isaac's "election" had an unusual side to it and felt more like rejection to him at the time!

Jacob was born, and as a result of his divine destiny, suffered years of rejection and hatred by his brother, as he himself was tested, humiliated and refined throughout his exile. Also, Joseph, Jacob's favored son whom God separated for greatness and authority, tasted rejection. His brothers' jealousy and hatred grew to murderous insanity as Joseph's awareness of his call and destiny increased! Indeed, their resentment reached that point of uncontrollable rage as rejection found full expression in the cry: "Kill him!"

From patriarch to patriarch, from generation to generation, the taste of rejection soaked deeper and deeper into the developing corporate soul of the nation of Israel. What God meant to be "set apart and chosen," the enemy distorted into being "resented and rejected."

After Jacob's family found temporary shelter in Egypt during Joseph's generation, hundreds of years of national slavery followed, offering no rights, no hopes and no escape. These conditions culminated in a national death sentence decreed by Pharaoh, who ordered all the male babies to be thrown into the crocodile-infested Nile River.

Can anyone fathom the depth of agony, the distress of soul, as they absorbed such rejection from their hosts while seemingly being forsaken by their God? And yet, it was precisely in these moments of desperation that they called upon the Lord and were heard in their distress, a historical pattern that continued from this point on.

Consider Israel's years in the wilderness as they emerged out of the Egyptian bondage and slavery, shaking off Pharaoh's yoke. Finally liberated from Pharaoh's slavery and free to worship God, they immediately began to draw hostility from the surrounding nations. With this newly acquired freedom came every unclean and heathen tribe in the region to nibble at Israel's heels in a hateful attempt to frustrate and discourage her. In her liberty, Israel was still resisted and rejected.

Surely, the nation brought many of these hardships upon herself, deserving the chastisement of a righteous, loving God. Historically, we see an ongoing theme of rejection penetrating deeply into the national consciousness, scarring it over and over again. No other nation on earth has known such repeated isolation and hatred for so long from other peoples. In fact, hardly any other nation has even existed for so long in order to accumulate such a tragic and lengthy past! And yet, they are the set-apart ones, the chosen, the elect! Could they ever reconcile these contradictions? Could they ever face their God again?

As history unfolds, Israel continues to be rejected, resisted, hated and attacked. Not only did neighboring nations, regional kingdoms, and world empires attempt to subdue, rape and enslave her, but her own prophets uttered divine judgments against her.

The worst of these prophecies might be Hosea's words to the unfaithful house of Israel, the Northern Kingdom: **"Because you have rejected knowledge, I also will reject you from being My priest"** (Hos 4:6). The nation's very identity, her call to be a priestly company before God on behalf of the rest of the nations (Ex 19:5-6), is now denied! Yet, how reassuring it is to recall God's eternal kindness and His faithfulness, for by the same prophet God declared Israel's ultimate restoration (Hosea 1:10,11; 14:1-9).

On the plateau of history, void of this divine revelation and of the Holy Spirit to interpret it, rejection sank deeper into the heart of the nation. And this, as any other principle of life, brings forth fruit after its own kind. Being saturated with it for generation after generation, the rejected nation adopted rejection as a way of life and a means of survival. When it becomes normal to be persecuted, one begins to expect it, and this very expectation breeds rejection. It was Job who confessed that **"what I fear comes upon me, and what I dread befalls me"** (Job 3:25). Indeed, as in a closed circuit, cause and effect give birth one to another. Thus, twisted social trends and cultural norms formed, as these dynamics of rejection and isolation interacted century after century, shaping the very soul of Israel and her contemporaries.

And, what can we say about the more recent history of Israel—the last two thousand years? We find that which was rooted as an integral component of the nation's soul kept continually manifesting.

After the destruction of the national life and the expulsion from the land, starting at A.D. 70, the Jewish refugees were driven from nation to nation. They were always on the move, never fully welcomed or accepted. In later centuries, persecution followed them wherever they went, especially after the reign of Emperor Constantine. He was the one who made Christianity the official religion of the Roman Empire during the fourth century A.D., which created the conditions for the church to plunge into a thousand years of spiritual darkness.

Imperial anti-Jewish legislation, backed by the false "Church Replacement Theology" taught by Augustine, paved the road of anti-Semitism and ushered in centuries of atrocities. These erroneous teachings, which have influenced the church ever since the third century A.D., basically conclude that God is finished with the natural Jew. They insist that all of God's wrath is upon the Jew, while all of His blessings are on the Gentile believer.

Over the centuries numerous persecutions and massacres ensued, leading to the crusaders' slaughter of tens of thousands of Jews in Christ's name while selling the survivors as slaves. The demonically trumped-up, blood-libel stories, falsely accusing Jews for murdering Christian children for their blood, swept through Europe, England and Spain for centuries, stirring the ignorant masses to murder. Thus, rejection reigned!

The Jews were blamed and persecuted for the Black Death plague in the fourteenth century which cut Europe's total population by one-third. They also were openly blasphemed and condemned by Martin Luther who, in his latter years, recommended to burn all their synagogues, raze and destroy their homes, and take from them their cash, silver and gold.

Down through the corridors of history, whether justified or unjustified, the people of Israel have lived with a perpetual and very real rejection complex. The rise of Nazi Germany and her diabolic treatment of the Jews was not at all atypical, but rather a natural fruit of the deep root of anti-Jewish prejudice and propaganda that spread throughout most of the continent. Every European nation, from Russia in the east to England in the west, at one time or another tolerated, and even advocated, Jewish persecution. England probably surpassed them all, with the exception of Germany, by denying Jewish refugees the right to find shelter in their homeland as they tried to escape Hitler's death camps during World War II. Again, God's chosen people were persecuted, hated and rejected to the utmost.

When Israel was finally granted back her land in 1948 and declared a sovereign state, there arose a great sigh of relief from the ancient and tired soul, but only for one day. The day following the Declaration of Independence, five hostile Arab armies attacked with the purpose of annihilating Israel, and the eight-month War of Independence was forced upon the young nation.

As the diabolic hatred continues to pour against Israel, vicious terrorist attacks persist and war follows war at the rate of more than one per decade. And as some Arab Middle Eastern leaders give full expression to the rage that burns against this chosen nation, world powers respond with cool diplomacy, often turning their face the other way.

Such isolation and such abuse for so long! How can any other people ever understand? No other nation on earth was called to carry such a burden throughout history. Indeed, David's cry is the nation's cry: **"For I am lonely and afflicted . . . bring me out of my distresses . . . Look upon my enemies . . . they hate me with violent hatred"** (Ps 25:16-19).

The Remedy

This stronghold of rejection and isolation was demonically induced, and in time undermined the call to be a set-apart people. It has so infiltrated the mind and soul of Israel that the nation is conditioned to doubt, suspect and question all others. Indeed, this stronghold not only blinded Israel for so long but has also paralyzed her heart from being able to respond to God's love.

The only remedy to heal a wounded heart is **love**, and the only weapon to dismantle a stronghold of rejection is **acceptance**—unconditional love and complete acceptance! Can we as Christians, who have received these graces from the Lord Himself, offer less to Israel?

For the Jews to properly respond to the gospel of God's Kingdom, they must first be accepted. The Lord Jesus Himself accepted sinners, received them with compassion to His bosom, and then called them to repent, to carry their cross, and follow Him. Indeed, the maturing church holds this key to Israel's heart. We believe it is one of the end-time keys to the liberating of the Jewish nation from deception, spiritual blindness and isolation.

Accept the Jew! Acknowledge what God has done in, through and for him. Learn to accept Israel as a real nation with real people, and not merely a "prophetic timepiece." The Lord did not suffer and die for "timepieces." He died to save souls—souls that are in dire need to be drawn back into His bosom through merciful acceptance.

Rejection is a type of death! Even as God labors to breathe life and resurrection upon Israel, Satan has built a wall of rejection around her. His strategy is to cut this one nation off from the other nations and from her call to serve them, but more than that to cut her off from God! The Accuser constantly whispers: "Did God separate you and set you apart? Then **be separated—be cut off!**"

This is the lie that only the maturing church can discern and tear down. And tear it down she will, employing spiritual warfare along with acts of love and acceptance.

The church is to walk into the reality of the Word of the Lord spoken by Jeremiah concerning the healing of Judah and Jerusalem: **"Behold, I will bring to it health and healing, and I will heal them; and I will reveal to them an abundance of peace and truth. And I will restore the fortunes of Judah and the fortunes of Israel, and I will rebuild them as they were at first . . . and I will pardon all their iniquities . . . And it [Jerusalem] shall be to Me a name of joy, praise, and glory before all the nations of the earth, which shall hear of all the good that I do for them"** (Jer 33:6-9).

We believe the future will bring many opportunities for powerful acts of love and reconciliation toward Israel and the Jewish people. What Europe saw as scattered acts of Christian virtue and sacrificial love during the Nazi holocaust will be multiplied many times in the days to come. **The maturing church is God's instrument of healing and restoration.** Will you avail your heart, your life and your hands for such a miracle?

SECTION FIVE:

The Prophetic Call

Introduction

"Now the Lord saw, and it was displeasing in His sight that there was no justice. And He saw that there was no man, and was astonished that there was no one to intercede; then His own arm brought salvation to Him; and His righteousness upheld Him" (Is 59:15-16).

The bottom line of all revelation is this: How does it affect our lives? How does it transform our souls? And how does it change us to be conformed to Jesus' image and purposes?

God requires of His people to not only agree with Him by way of granting mental ascent to His Word, but to be yoked with Him in the bringing forth of His purposes. Thus, those who are in Christ are called to rediscover their identity and destiny in Him, and to find practical means by which to serve Him.

23

The Church's Response

Every genuine work of God involves the planting of the seed, the season of gestation, travail and labor and, only then, the birthing of the new creation. As we consider the advent of the church of the Lord Jesus upon the earth following His resurrection, we must recognize that this church did not "drop from heaven," nor was it formed in a vacuum. Indeed, the church, the company of the redeemed who were washed by the blood and sanctified by the Spirit, was **born!**

The Womb

The birth of the church necessitated the birthing process in its entirety. The divine seed, the Messiah, had to be entrusted to an earthen womb. This womb in which He grew, and out of which the church came forth, was none other than the national frame of Israel.

While many acknowledge Israel's physical exile of the last nineteen hundred years, only a few recognize that the nation also experienced a spiritual exile as well. The calling, the exclusive standing with God, and the anointing were now extended to another people group, as the "baton" was handed down to the apostles. Out of Israel God birthed a younger agency through which to further demonstrate His kindness and grace to a lost world. Thus, the church was grafted into Israel's role as priest over the nations while the Jewish nation itself was "sent to the bench."

As in any birth, the intensifying contractions, the trauma, and the laying down of one's life took their toll as the church was being birthed. Israel, now an exhausted and bloody womb, collapsed and was taken out of the way. The young church, vibrant and anointed, spread herself across the heathen nations, bearing the life of heaven in her wings. But what about the old womb? It was not to be forsaken forever, was it? **"God has not rejected His people, has He? May it never be!"** (Rom 11:1)

That ancient womb is to rise one last time upon the face of the earth in order to give birth to the last of God's new creation, even as it did the first! Yet, this very nation that once gave birth—now is in need herself to be birthed by another. Who will provide the womb?

The Prophetic Breath

It is imperative to understand that Israel's rejection and restoration manifest in two phases. As she was exiled from both her physical **and** spiritual inheritance, so she is being restored today in both the physical **and** the spiritual realms. One of the clearest scriptural pictures of this two-phase restoration is found in the prophecy of Ezekiel, chapter 37.

The prophet, facing the horrible sight of a valley filled with lifeless, hopeless and disjointed dry bones, is commanded by God to prophesy recovery to them. **"Prophesy over these bones, and say to them, 'O dry bones, hear the word of the Lord'** . . . **'Behold, I will cause breath to enter you that you may come to life. And I will put sinews on you, make flesh grow back on you, cover you with skin, and put breath in you that you may come alive; and you will know that I am the Lord' "** (Ez 37:4-6).

Indeed, the scriptures prophesied both physical and spiritual healing for Israel, yet clearly, the physical came first. **"And I looked, and behold, sinews were on them, and flesh grew, and skin covered them"** (Ez 37:8). And although the spiritual healing is the end result, the natural must precede it (1 Cor 15:46). These bones, which are **"the whole house of Israel"** (Ez 37:11), responded to the Word of the Lord and gained a bodily resurrection.

However, the prophet discerned with alarm that, though these bones arose from their corporate grave with a new purpose, **"there was no breath in them"** (Ez 37:8), and the actual description in verse 9 is that they were still as **"slain."** The original Hebrew text, **"Harrogim,"** denotes "those who are killed, dead beyond hope." Indeed, the natural restoration of Israel, though miraculous and awesome, is only a partial one.

The prophetic process reached a "halfway" point in verse 8, and we find the nation suspended—alive in the natural, yet without life in the spirit. This condition describes precisely the state of the Jewish people in this century. In the natural dimension there has been a great coming together with all the evidence of physical life. Yet, in the spiritual dimension, there still is blindness and hardness of heart.

God responds to the prophet's cry, saying, **"Prophesy to the breath, prophesy, son of man, and say ... 'Thus says the Lord God, "Come from the four winds, O breath, and breathe on these slain, that they come to life" ' "** (Ez 37:9). Obediently, the prophet prophesies as he was commanded, and **"the breath came into them, and they came to life, and stood on their feet, an exceedingly great army"** (Ez 37:10).

To these restored people the Word of God continues to come, saying, **"Behold, I will open your graves and cause you to come up out of your graves, My people; and I will bring you into the land of Israel ... And I will put My Spirit within you, and you will come to life, and I will place you on your own land"** (Ez 37:12-14). In these words God promises nothing short of the miracle of resurrection life as He imparts His Spirit to the regathered nation.

Still, this promise of spiritual revival hinges upon the raising and completion of the ministry of this prophetic **son of man company**, who is to prophesy the life-giving Word of God to Israel. Today, the

Lord is calling forth this company of intercessors to corporately prophesy and speak to Israel's lifeless, hopeless, dry bones until the vision is completed. And, undoubtedly, the Lord in His wisdom and sovereignty is calling upon the true church of Jesus to carry Israel in her womb of intercession, laboring over this "historic baby" until it is safely born.

24

The Friend

Ample evidence testifies to the fact that it was the intercession and travail of God's faithful servants which supported, guided and inspired many of modern Israel's leaders. From the early days of the Zionistic revival to the present-day affairs of the state of Israel, prayers of compassion, filled with faith, helped shape Israel's history. Heroes whose names never made the headlines, yet are forever recorded in heaven, contributed much to the momentum and strength of Israel's restoration.

One such prophetic hero was a British officer named Ord Wingate, serving in what was then called "Palestine" during the British Mandate between the two World Wars. The region was administered by England, who was commissioned by the League of Nations to prepare it as a national home for the Jewish people. Much turmoil and violence flooded the land at this time, as Arab hostilities intensified against the young Jewish settlements, harassing even the British presence.

Wingate was not only a British officer but also a Christian officer, enlisted in the army of the King of kings. He was known for his unique and nonconforming personality, his great devotion to the Bible, and his passion for Zionism! He understood God's plan for the Jewish people, and he loved the land of Israel. In fact, many times he walked the length and the breadth of the land all by himself, discovering, exploring and delighting himself in her, as he envisioned and relived famous biblical battles.

At some point during his tour of duty, Wingate felt called to help raise and train a Jewish army, an underground force that could successfully defend the Jewish settlements and deter Arab hostilities which were on the rise. Defense was the only strategy the settlers implemented against the murderous Arab gangs. An offensive approach was not in their vocabulary. Wingate was determined to change that.

Having his heart fixed on the divine purpose, Wingate went on to invest himself, his experience, and his military expertise in the young Jewish soldiers he recruited from the underground organizations. After winning the trust of the leaders of the Jewish community, Wingate went on to train these highly motivated, yet poorly equipped, fighters.

They met in secret, and their training often took place at night. Weaponry, personal discipline and ethics, battle strategy, and physical fitness were only a part of his agenda. And so zealous and convicted was this man of the biblical and prophetic rightness of his activities that nothing could stop him.

His early "disciples" recall being trained by him in the hills of lower Galilee. In the darkness of night he would command and lead them in attacking enemy encampments, breaking the backbone of the great "Arab Riot" and bringing to an end the murderous campaigns against the expanding Jewish settlements. Carrying his open Bible in his hand, he would quote scriptures to them, exclaiming, **"Run, you lions of Judah, mount up, you sons of Joseph!"** And indeed, for him this was the fulfillment of a divine commission, as he believed that the Lord, His God, sent him to raise up and train the Israeli warriors to the stature of their great Hebrew forefathers.

Indeed, these early disciples of Wingate became some of the chief leaders and commanders of the Israeli Defense Force. This

God-sent Englishman not only trained and taught them how to fight, he, in fact, **breathed** upon them the breath of life! He, as well as many others, played a part in the **son of man company** who prophesies over the dry bones, calling them to life again!

The fact was that his trainees were not only unskilled and poorly equipped, but were descendants of a race which had no military experience for the last 1,900 years. During the centuries of dispersion, the Jewish people lost all knowledge of warfare, self-defense, and even the unction to fight! **What Wingate did spiritually was no less than to participate in the re-creating of the warrior heart of Israel!**

His life and deeds are recorded in a small book published in Hebrew and titled *The Friend*. And indeed, what greater compliment, what higher more noble title, can the regathered Jew bestow upon a Christian witness but that of "friend"? After centuries of disillusionment and suffering by the hands of so-called Christians, it was in this century that God's grace began to draw closer the true Christian and the Jew in the embrace of restoration and prophetic fulfillment.

Such are the ways of our God. Wingate lost his life on some long-forgotten battlefield in Africa. His name has long been erased from even the memory of his own country, yet it will never be erased from the chronicles of God which recall the going forth of this spirit of love and faith for Israel's sake.

25

Ruth—The Prophetic Womb

The Old Testament provides us with magnificent prophetic pictures depicting spiritual truths. Indeed, as it has been said concerning God's Covenants, "The New is concealed in the Old and the Old is revealed in the New." Likewise, we find numerous texts in the Old Testament scriptures that, while depicting a very real and earthly episode, are nevertheless prophetically pointing toward the great fulfillment which is in the Messiah and the Kingdom of God. The story of Ruth is one such picture where we find an end-time revelation of the role of the true church in the restoration of Israel.

This ancient story unfolds in the days of the Judges. This was a time of much confusion and turmoil in Israel, with only temporary periods of peace and prosperity. As famine plagued the land of Judah, a family from Bethlehem, which ironically means "House of Bread" in the Hebrew language, went to sojourn in the land of Moab, a Gentile pagan society.

Breaking the Mosaic law, this Jewish family left their inheritance to look for provision among the Gentiles. The head of the household, Elimelech, which in Hebrew translates "My God is King," died. The two sons died as well, fulfilling their own prophetic names, Mahlon and Chilion, meaning "Sickly" and "Pining Away." These are two of the curses pronounced by Moses over the Israelites as punishment if they would go out to sojourn among the pagan nations.

Naomi, the mother, is our key character. Prophetically, she typifies the nation of Israel in that, while in spiritual famine and drought, she left her land to sojourn among the nations. Cut off from her land, void of the covering of God, her husband (Elimelech), and of the future promise and protection of her offspring (Mahlon and Chilion), Naomi is left alone with her two Gentile daughters-in-law.

The name of one is Orpah, meaning "The Back of One's Neck." The name of the other is Ruth, meaning "Friend and Comrade." These two women prophetically typify two kinds of churches—the one that will turn its back on old, desperate Israel, and the other which will be her friend. Both were married into the covenant people, but only one lived up to her vows!

Test of Devotion

Good news traveled fast, and word came to Naomi that the famine in Judah was over. Having no reason to dwell any longer in the land of Moab, she prepared for her return to the homeland. And, it was at this juncture that both her daughters-in-law were to fulfil their prophetic names.

Though walking with her mother-in-law for some distance, Orpah soon turned her back on Naomi, while Ruth continued on, clinging to her mother-in-law. Three times Naomi had urged them to depart from her and return to their own people and culture. Three times Ruth withstood the temptation to withdraw and, therefore, passed the test of loyalty.

In fact, as Ruth gave expression to her commitment to old and helpless Naomi, she said, "Do not urge me to leave you or turn back from following you; for where you go, I will go, and where you lodge, I will lodge. Your people shall be my people, and your God, my

God" (Ruth 1:16). Unlike her sister-in-law, who returned **"to her people and her GODS"** (Ruth 1:15, emphasis mine), Ruth gave a clear confession of her devotion to Naomi's people **and** Naomi's God.

Indeed, the sober admonition of this Old Testament allegory points to the danger awaiting those who do not find it in their hearts to remain loyal to the people and the God of Israel. For, in this symbolic analogy, we find that such persons or groups will surely return, not only to their own **people**, but also to their previous **gods**, as did Orpah. And, though the New Covenant reality is much broader and grace-filled than the Old Covenant's types, we, nevertheless, must draw honest conclusions. For indeed, **"these things happened to them as an example, and they were written for our instruction, upon whom the ends of the ages have come"** (1 Cor 10:11).

In addition, we recognize that, while down through the centuries myriads of Christians have joyfully expressed their devotion and commitment to the God of Israel, they nevertheless disregarded and rejected His ancient people. Judging from this scriptural text, we find that embracing the One must include the other as well! As Ruth clung to the people, she could, therefore, cling to their God.

Ruth continued to proclaim her devotion, saying, **"Where you die, I will die, and there I will be buried. Thus may the Lord do to me, and worse, if anything but death parts you and me"** (Ruth 1:17). Today we use these words in marriage ceremonies, demonstrating the depth and degree of devotion between husband and wife. However, these words were originally spoken between two women. One was born into the covenant of God, the other entered it through marriage.

Back Home

As the two weary travelers entered the territory of Judah, it was at **"the beginning of barley harvest"** (Ruth 1:22). This significant timing of the natural harvest serves to point to the greater spiritual harvest when Jew and Gentile unite in purpose and ministry to see God's greatest move on earth before the end of this age.

The status of the two women was that of refugees, as all of Naomi's possessions and property were lost, and their only livelihood was found in gleaning the fields. The old and disillusioned woman now changed her name from Naomi, which means "**Pleasant,**" to Mara, which in the Hebrew language means "**Bitter.**" In answering the puzzled women who welcomed them in Bethlehem, Naomi exclaimed, "**Do not call me Naomi; call me Mara, for the Almighty has dealt very bitterly with me ... Why do you call me Naomi, since the Lord has witnessed against me and the Almighty has afflicted me?**" (Ruth 1:20-21)

Indeed, this bitterness of soul and disappointment of heart was Israel's condition as she returned from her exile to the devastations of the ancient homeland. Though the homecoming was sweet, the harsh reality of the present conditions and the great loss, isolation and suffering overwhelmed her soul.

God's Redemption

The story unfolds and, prophetically, Ruth finds herself gleaning in the fields of Boaz. The name Boaz means, "**In Him There is Strength.**" He was the **kinsman-redeemer** who, according to Israel's law, was the only man who had the legal right to redeem the name and the property of the deceased. Being an unmarried man, Boaz could also restore the hope of future descendants by marrying the widow of the deceased, which he, indeed, went on to do.

Ruth's humility and faithfulness attracted the attention of Boaz, and he declared, "**All that you have done for your mother-in-law after the death of your husband has been fully reported to me**" (Ruth 2:11). This kinsman-redeemer began to love her for her kindness and servanthood toward old, embittered Naomi, who could offer Ruth no reward in return for her devotion.

This prophetic scenario reached its climax as Ruth captured the redeemer's heart, and he took her as his bride. Interestingly, in the process of them being drawn one to another, old Naomi offered young Ruth both counsel and instruction, saying, "**Wash yourself therefore, and anoint yourself and put on your best clothes, and go down to the threshing floor . . . go and uncover his feet and lie down; then he will tell you what you shall do**" (Ruth 3:3-4). Indeed, fatigued and embittered as she may be, ancient Israel can still offer counsel and wisdom to the young and vibrant bride-to-be as she approaches her Beloved!

The scripture testifies that "she became his wife, and he went in to her. And the Lord enabled her to conceive, and she gave birth to a son" (Ruth 4:13). Strategically, Ruth's womb was opened by the Lord at this time, for Ruth was not a virgin; she was a widow who had known a man before, yet bore no children. Rather, her womb had been closed until her marriage to the appointed man, the kinsman-redeemer.

Likewise, the true church bears no spiritual offspring unless she is intimately united with the Lord. Down through the centuries the church has flirted with and was adulterously related to other masters, but now at the end of this age, she is beginning to prepare herself for her True Husband, the great kinsman-redeemer.

The Promised Seed

And, who was this son Ruth gave birth to? Who was this male child of whom the neighbor women said, "A son has been born to Naomi!" (Ruth 4:17) How could they say that old and lifeless Naomi has now given birth to this child? Boaz was not Naomi's husband, nor was it her womb that brought forth the boy. Yet the prophetic declaration was that the child was born to Naomi!

The prophetic fact was that young and loving Ruth offered her vibrant and fruitful womb so that old and lifeless Naomi could have a male child one last time! A son was now present to resurrect and preserve the family name and blood line!

And as the women said to Naomi, "Blessed is the Lord who has not left you without a redeemer today . . . may he also be to you a restorer of life and a sustainer of your old age; for your daughter-in-law, who loves you and is better to you than seven sons, has given birth to him" (Ruth 4:14-15). And significantly, the scripture testifies that "Naomi took the child and laid him in her lap, and became his nurse" (Ruth 4:16). The scriptural suggestion here is that Naomi actually began to nurse the child, a biological provision that was not uncommon to their culture.

Who was this son? And what name did they give him, but "Obed, He is the father of Jesse, the father of David" (Ruth 4:17). Obed means "A Worker; Servant," one who perfectly does the will of him who sends him.

The real miracle, however, was that Naomi, holding her God-given grandson, now assumed responsibility and cloaked herself again with a maternal garment as she cared for her offspring. Another miracle took place in Ruth's heart as she laid down her rights and natural instincts for her firstborn in favor of her mother-in-law.

From Type to Reality

There is a young and loving church whom God is calling forth these days to lend her womb as a birthing chamber of travail. Old and exhausted Israel must bear a son and be fruitful once more, yet has no life within herself to do so.

In keeping with the prophetic nature of this story, we recognize that the son who was born to Naomi, **Obed**, the perfect servant, testifies to the virtue and quality of character which will be evident in Israel's last generation. This nation is destined to give birth one last time at the end of this age. And, just as that which she gave birth to in the first century—the Messiah—transformed the world, so shall it be in the last century.

Hear this cry: **"We were pregnant, we writhed in labor, we gave birth, as it were, only to wind. We could not accomplish deliverance for the earth nor were inhabitants of the world born"** (Is 26:18). This is Israel's historical trauma and cry. The nation that was called to represent God, to accomplish deliverance for the nations, and to be a blessing to all the families of the earth is crying intensely in frustration. All her labors, her sacrifice and her suffering for century after century have produced absolutely nothing. The six million Jews who died in the holocaust brought no deliverance for the earth, and forty-five years of national suffering and hardship since 1948 gave birth, as it were, only to wind!

Nothing was accomplished toward Israel's mission to the nations that was visible to the natural eye. To the undiscerning heart, her historic saga of pain and endless persecutions bore no fruit at all. And yet, the same scripture continues in the promise that, **"Your dead will live; their corpses will rise. You who lie in the dust, awake and shout for joy, for your dew is as the dew of the dawn, and the earth will give birth to the departed spirits"** (Is 26:19). Indeed, there is a hope and a promise of resurrection life for and through the old lifeless vessel—but not without a fruitful womb!

Be a Ruth

Pray for the Spirit to come from the four corners of the earth and revive the ancient people. Pray for the church to stand with and faithfully uphold Israel in love and intercession. And notice, in this prophetic scenario, how young Ruth could only find her lover and her husband as she joined herself to Naomi, thus covenanting herself to the ancient people and their destiny. Indeed, the bride of Christ will find and unite with her promised Bridegroom as she ministers to Israel, gleaning in the fields of Bethlehem.

Isaiah describes Israel's amazement as she beholds her end-time children miraculously gathered unto her: **"Then you will say in your heart, 'Who has begotten these for me, since I have been bereaved of my children, and am barren, an exile and a wanderer? And who has reared these? Behold, I was left alone; From where did these come?' "** (Is 49:21)

Indeed, this miracle of both the natural and spiritual awakenings takes place as Ruth, the loving, humble church, positions herself sacrificially in a posture of labor, preparing to give birth to "Naomi's last son." Thus God's final purposes in this age will come to pass.

Israel is in need of a womb—a living, loving, life-giving womb. Will the church be **"Orpah"** or **"Ruth"**? Is your church becoming a **"leaver"** or a **"cleaver"**? Do we possess the heart of an **abortionist** or a **midwife**?

The line of revelation and commitment to God's purpose with Israel is being drawn these very days in the heart of Christendom. Compromise and fence-riding will not be tolerated on this issue much longer, as the stakes are too high, and the consequences will mean either eternal glory or shame.

This is our prophetic environment today: Naomi is returning back to Bethlehem, leaning on Ruth's strong arm. The fields are rich with harvest ready to be reaped, and Boaz is waiting in the midst of it all. And, as Jew and Gentile, Boaz and Ruth, unite in marriage and harmonize in God's eternal purpose, they will give birth to the **one new man generation.**

26

Esther—The Bride in Intercession

An Introductory Note

The story of Esther offers us a profound picture in types and shadows of the intercession of the bride of Christ on behalf of Israel and the Jewish people. It will be helpful in gleaning the prophetic significance for you to read the book of Esther afresh before continuing in this chapter.

In this Old Testament scenario, we find amazing prophetic types: Ahasuerus, the sovereign king, portraying our sovereign God, reigns over his mighty kingdom of many peoples. Amongst these people is a remnant of the people of Israel, which speaks of our present age. Vashti, the queen, represents a prideful and disobedient church which falls from her lofty position. Mordecai is seen in the role of the Holy Spirit, leading, training and exhorting the intercessors. Haman and his plan to annihilate the Jewish people demonstrate the ever-present anti-Semitic and anti-Israeli diabolic drive. And Esther, the beautiful and willing maiden, is a type of the bride of Christ, the glorious church, in intercession.

Apart from the intercessory ministry of the Lord Jesus Himself, we cannot find in God's Word a more dramatic, dangerous and successful intercession than that of Esther. Among the great intercessors of the Bible, no other portrays so clearly and vividly the position and the ministry of the true church toward God on behalf of the Jewish people.

The Setting of the Stage

At the time of this story, King Ahasuerus of Persia reigned supreme over most of the then-known world, exercising utmost authority over 127 states. This indivisible number speaks of the totality, strength, and all-encompassing nature of his kingdom. Indeed, a mighty throne that was!

Vashti, the queen, was no doubt an impressive figure. Her very name means "beautiful woman" in the ancient Persian tongue, and her position was one of great privilege and authority before the sovereign king. She resembles a particular type of church—one of great pomp, pride and august appearance. Yet all of her outward splendor and great position availed her not on the day she disobeyed her husband, the king.

During a great royal feast, seven eunuchs were sent from the presence of Ahasuerus with an urgent and commanding invitation for his queen to appear before him, that he might display her beauty to his court. These seven eunuchs represent the all-compelling divine call to come into the presence of God!

"**But Queen Vashti refused**" (Esther 1:12). Ridiculing the king's command and disobeying his expressed will, the queen found herself deposed, divorced, and ultimately replaced. A royal edict was issued declaring that, "**Vashti should come no more into the presence of King Ahasuerus, and let the king give her royal position to another who is more worthy than she**" (Esther 1:19).

A search was conducted throughout the whole kingdom for a virgin who would be worthy to become the king's bride; and a most thorough and careful search it was. Indeed, a bride was found for the mighty king. Esther was chosen to join the king's harem, entering a season of preparation and beautification before she could be presented to him.

This beautiful Jewish maiden, void of earthly parents, was raised by her righteous uncle, Mordecai, in a low and humble estate. Though dwelling among the pagans, her roots and true identity were with the people of Israel. Her very name means "star" and speaks of her high calling, even her destiny, for heavenly purposes. She reminds us of yet another kind of church—this one possessing hidden qualities, humility, and a noble spirit.

The excellency of her character and her inner beauty, all wrapped in a delightful vessel, quickly won her favor among the other maidens and the eunuchs in the king's harem. Esther's humility was her strength, as we see that, during the period of her preparation, **"she did not request anything except what Hegai, the king's eunuch who was in charge of the women, advised"** (Esther 2:15).

She also kept secret her true identity at Mordecai's command and found great confidence in her submission to him. Her heart was at rest, having no need for self-promotion or striving after position. Indeed, **"Esther found favor in the eyes of all who saw her"** (Esther 2:15).

In considering Mordecai's role typifying that of the Holy Spirit, we find his place in Esther's life as one of a righteous, holy and faceless influence. He is the one in charge of nurturing, tutoring and instructing the bride, as she prepares herself for her high calling. In spite of Esther's increasing power in the king's harem and the inherent temptations of her newly acquired and privileged position, she **"did what Mordecai told her as she had done when under his care"** (Esther 2:20). Again, humility and submission were the secret of her great favor and promotion.

After the customary season of beautification was completed (six months with oil of myrrh and six months with spices and cosmetics, symbolizing the anointing of God and the various gifts and flavors He pours into a yielded vessel), the young maiden was presented to the sovereign king. **"And the king loved Esther more than all the women, and she found favor and kindness with him more than all the virgins, so that he set the royal crown on her head and made her queen instead of Vashti"** (Esther 2:17).

The stage was set. The main players were positioned to act out their prophetic roles—when evil entered! A diabolic plan stirred by jealousy and unrestrained hatred was devised against the Jewish people in the king's realm. The anti-Jewish spirit of rejection and murder found full expression once again against Israel, as Haman took offense because **"Mordecai neither bowed down nor paid homage"** to him (Esther 3:2).

And so Haman qualified himself to become the chief instrument of wickedness in the Devil's plan to annihilate the Jewish population. The sovereign king himself permitted and legalized this evil, and a decree was issued for the destruction of the Jewish people.

What horrible fate came upon them overnight as dark clouds of gloom and despair once again converged upon this people. How they probably wished they would have returned earlier to the desolate land of Judah with Zurubbabel. How they must have questioned, again, "Why us?" Once more, as history unfolded, it seemed the whole world turned into a monster to devour and destroy the seed of Israel. Global powers decreed their annihilation, and there was no escape.

The battle was over the very existence of the Jewish people, the covenant God made with their fathers, and His promises to their descendants. Blows were exchanged between Haman and Mordecai in this struggle as to who would influence the throne. Haman was the accuser, while Esther was the instrument of intercession. King Ahasuerus himself was the supreme and sovereign judge who would determine the final outcome.

The War of the Ages

Notably, as we trace Haman's roots, we find that he was a descendant of the Agagite (Esther 3:1). This ancestor of his was none other than Agag, king of Amalek, Israel's ancient and implacable foe. Mordecai, as we find in Esther 2:5, is traced to Kish, a Benjamite, from whose loins came King Saul of Israel.

Concerning the Amalekites, who had been hostile to Israel ever since the early years of the exodus from Egypt, God commanded King Saul, **"I will punish Amalek for what he did to Israel, how he set himself against him on the way while he was coming up from Egypt. Now go and strike Amalek and utterly destroy all that he** has, and do not spare him; but put to death both man and woman, child and infant, ox and sheep, camel and donkey" (1 Sam 15:2-3).

King Saul, however, compromised and did not utterly destroy his enemy! In disobedience to God's Word, he spared the spoils of war, the livestock, and the life of King Agag himself. As a result, not only was Saul himself rejected from the throne (1 Sam 15:22-23), but Amalek was allowed posterity, though Agag himself was slain by Samuel, the prophet.

Thus, because of Saul's disobedience, Amalek was not brought to an end. Future generations of Amalek continued to be fueled by diabolic hatred, and the campaign against the people of God continued. And now, in the time of Esther, we find Mordecai and Haman, the very kin of both Saul and Agag, locked once again in this battle of the ages. **Indeed, our failure to fully execute God's judgment over evil will only perpetuate its impact!**

"For Such a Time as This"

Because of Haman's high position in the king's court, there was only one person in the kingdom who could stand in the gap to intercede. Should Esther choose to, she could make the difference, as she was the bride, the most excellent of all maidens, and the king's beloved queen. She was the only one who had access to both the king's chamber and his heart, and being of Jewish descent herself, she was her people's only hope.

Mordecai, as a type of the Holy Spirit, was greatly grieved. When he learned of the evil plan, he **"tore his clothes, put on sackcloth and ashes, and went out into the midst of the city and wailed loudly and bitterly"** (Esther 4:1). Indeed, the grief of the Holy Spirit is often great and will be cast as a burden into the midst of a caring people. God is not embarrassed by the truth, but rather He exposes it for the purpose of identification and intercession.

Mordecai, refusing to be superficially comforted and swayed from his purpose, proceeded to instruct Esther in the battle strategy. In fact, he went on **"to order her to go in to the king to implore his favor and to plead with him for her people"**! (Esther 4:8)

This intercession had to be an act of complete abandonment, as none could enter uninvited into the presence of the great king without risking their lives—not even the queen herself! For indeed, "**any man or woman who comes to the king to the inner court who is not summoned, he has but one law, that he be put to death, unless the king holds out to him the golden scepter so that he may live**" (Esther 4:11).

Though Esther's heart was fearful and uncertain, the command of the Spirit prevailed as Mordecai's warning came sternly: "**Do not imagine that you in the king's palace can escape any more than all the Jews. For if you remain silent at this time, relief and deliverance WILL arise for the Jews from another place and you and your father's house will perish**" (Esther 4:13-14, emphasis mine).

This intercession could cost the bride her very life, for she not only would enter the king's chamber uninvited, but also would openly identify herself with those already doomed for destruction! From her exalted and protected position, the queen would have to stoop low, partaking in the grief and despair of the Jewish suffering, exposing her roots and true identity as one with them.

Either the bride would be swept away by the evil and murderous flood already rushing to consume them, or they all would receive grace, mercy and deliverance out of the cup of her royalty. Which would it be?

Esther, who stands for the bride of Christ in this prophetic picture, was reminded of her destiny. The Spirit spoke, "**And who knows whether you have not attained royalty for such a time as this?**" (Esther 4:14)

The Bride in Action

In preparation for her warfare, Esther called for prayer and fasting: "**Go, assemble all the Jews who are found in Susa, and fast for me . . . for three days . . . I and my maidens also will fast . . . And thus I will go in to the king, which is not according to the law; and if I perish, I perish**" (Esther 4:16). Now that the bride was moving in the will of God and in submission to His purpose, she had authority to summon a national fast to prepare her way.

It is significant that Esther's access to the king was "**not according to the law**"! This act of bold and selfless intercession, endangering her own interests and life, was not based on legal rights or political manipulations. Her entry into the king's chamber was founded only upon her relationship with him! Apart from true devotion, mutual respect and love, she would lose her position and her head!

After the days of fasting ended, Esther put on her royal robes and came in to the king. **"And it happened when the king saw Esther the queen standing in the court, she obtained favor in his sight; and the king extended to Esther the golden scepter which was in his hand. So Esther came near and touched the top of the scepter"** (Esther 5:2). Having gained access to his chamber and to his heart, the bride now began her powerful intercession.

From that position of acceptance, Esther implemented the plan of action she received during her time of fasting. With confidence she moved to draw out the enemy, to expose his motive, and then to silence him. And indeed, before the presence of the mighty king the vileness of Haman was brought to full light, and the wickedness of his intentions laid bare. Haman was found guilty and delivered to be hanged unto death on the very gallows he prepared for Mordecai.

The king then issued a second decree superseding the first one which authorized the annihilation of the Jewish people. This second decree now authorized and deputized these very victims to rise up, assemble together, pursue and destroy their enemies! (Esther 8:11)

In fact, the king's first decree brought to full exposure and flushed out the enemies of the Jews, so that they themselves might be destroyed by their intended victims at the second decree! **The prey were given authority to become the predators!**

Not only was the intercession successful in averting the evil plan, but also Mordecai (as the Spirit) was now restored to his proper position. **"Then Mordecai went out from the presence of the king in royal robes of blue and white, with a large crown of gold and a garment of fine linen and purple; and the city of Susa shouted and rejoiced. For the Jews there was light and gladness and joy and honor. And in each and every province . . . there was gladness and joy for the Jews . . . And many among the peoples of the land BECAME JEWS, for the dread of the Jews had fallen on them"** (Esther 8:15-17, emphasis mine).

Indeed, where the praying church takes her position sacrificially and boldly, there the Holy Spirit is honored and revered, and the people enjoy liberty, great gladness and light. Many will then be caught in the net of the great harvest, joining themselves to the household of God in the fear and the joy of the Lord.

And thus, the story nears its end with great victory and deliverance. We see how the sovereign king granted the bride's petition and request. We see how all these things worked out for good for those who loved God and remained true to His purposes. And yet, this great lesson of intercession still stands to be fulfilled one last time.

A bride, most excellent of all maidens, prepared and perfected for royalty, is yet to stand in the presence of the supreme authority and make powerful, all-demanding intercession on behalf of the persecuted Jew! **The fate of the people will again rest in the hand of the bride.**

As to the rest of the story—the victory of the Jews, the utter destruction of their enemies, the glory of Esther, and the exaltation of Mordecai—let us continue to press in with the Lord as He Himself watches over His Word to fulfill it.

27

Weep Not for Rachel

As some of our friends know, our daughter Rachel went to be with the Lord on Friday, March 22, 1991, at five weeks of age. Rachel's life was, and still is, an act of intercession.

Rachel was conceived in Israel during the early summer of 1990, when we were on a visit to the homeland, and was carried in the womb full term even as Israel is carried in the womb of intercession by those who love her. A number of witnesses, prophetic dreams, and words of knowledge came prior to her birth, testifying to the purpose of her life. Some we understood; some could only come to light when we looked back.

The labor and delivery took place during the Persian Gulf War of 1991, and were surrounded by and immersed in the trauma, deep concern and travail that filled our souls during those difficult days. As missiles were dropping on Israel's civilian population, some of them hitting my parents' neighborhood outside Tel Aviv, Rachel was born. We knew this child stood for Israel, again drinking from her cup of sorrows, again engulfed in hatred and rejection. Yet the child was born!

During the last and most severe blast of winter, when temperatures plunged overnight to twenty below zero, with high winds and deadly wind-chill, Rachel came into this world. As the Spirit had spoken to us earlier, she came during this terrible storm when the elements were crashing violently and the winds were howling outside. Yet, as promised, a most wonderful and tangible peace filled our home during labor and birth.

If the child had been a boy, his name would have been Israel. But she was a girl, and the Lord named her Rachel. A lamb. Though just a tiny baby, it became increasingly evident to us that her heart was crying out to God continuously. And, while she was a normal and healthy baby, when looking into this world she found no comfort for her soul. Even at her mother's breast, there was that search and longing for a better world, and her pure and tiny wail still echoes in our hearts until today.

Rachel came with us to Kansas City in March 1991, as we were holding one of our intercession conferences concerning Israel and the church. It seemed her grief increased as we neared the city, and there are no better words to describe what took place in her soul than to recall the Lord's increasing grief and pain as He was nearing Jerusalem for the last time. She had an appointment with her destiny there.

As I was sharing the heart of the revelation concerning the Gentile church giving birth to Israel in prayer, I pointed to Rachel. "Her soul," I said, "is in such desperate need for God that it has brought us to a place of intercession we have not known before with any of our other children. She is like Israel," I told the conference, "who, without the church travailing and the power of God being released, would not find healing and divine life in her desperate need."

We had recognized by this time that Rachel's life conveyed a prophetic burden, portraying the tender birthing of Israel before the Lord. Yet, I had no idea how painfully true and Spirit-led was my illustration. That very night the Lord took Rachel back to Himself.

At the crack of dawn the angel of the Lord silently descended and scooped up her little soul, taking her home; her warfare was accomplished, her soul satisfied. The peace encompassing her crib and the smile on her lips when we found her cold body in the morning were from another realm.

We knew Rachel was gone, but still had to go through the proper medical procedures. The hospital staff gave up after nearly an hour of intense attempts to revive her little body, leaving her in my arms. My friend Mike Bickle and I, through our tears, asked the Father one last time for resurrection life, then gave her back to Him. His will for her life was accomplished, and He called her back to Himself.

The previous night we had taught from the book of Ruth, seeing how this Gentile daughter-in-law of Naomi was, in fact, a type of the church. And, as we departed from the hospital that morning, we left Rachel's little body in the arms of a beautiful, black nurse whose tears mingled with ours. Her name was **Naomi.** Indeed, the kindness of the Lord and His gentle hand covered over our pain.

As we returned home with empty arms to our awaiting girls and the heartbroken church in Cedar Rapids, Iowa, a song was sung for us at the Sunday morning service; that song was given to our musicians by revelation on the date of Rachel's birth five weeks earlier.

They sang, " **'A voice is heard in Ramah, lamentation and bitter weeping. Rachel is weeping for her children; she refuses to be comforted for her children, because they are no more.' Thus says the Lord, 'Restrain your voice from weeping, and your eyes from tears; for your work shall be rewarded,' declares the Lord, 'And they shall return from the land of the enemy. And there is hope for your future,' declares the Lord, 'and your children shall return to their own territory' "** (Jer 31:15-17).

Thus, the Lord Himself, by His Spirit, placed His seal upon her life. His triumphant declaration in song over Rachel was that her weeping and pain will be no more, for her work shall be rewarded. The costly intercession and sacrificial travail which is constantly rising before the throne of our God will bear fruit! And every seed sown into the rich soil of God's promises will surely blossom!

Weep not for Rachel. For, **"From the mouth of infants and nursing babes Thou hast established strength, because of Thine adversaries, to make the enemy and the revengeful cease"** (Ps 8:2).

Rachel's life was her warfare; her departure was a declaration from the Lord. So sobering came the word of God through her; so solemn was His act.

Thus, we offer praise and gratitude to the God of all flesh, who does all things well. We are thankful for having carried Rachel full term in the womb, and then five weeks in our arms. We offer her warfare and intercession as incense upon the ancient stone-built altar of Israel, and we anticipate our reunion with her in the presence of the Lord.

Concluding Appeal

We do not know the cost of purchasing God's healing for Israel. We do know it won't be cheap. Our daughter Rachel fell in battle as seed into the ground and died, that she might bring forth a hundredfold. And our prayer and faith toward God is for the sacrifice of this little lamb to stir and empower holy and mighty intercession in the heart of the church on behalf of Israel.

As imperfect as this book may be, you now possess more insight and information than before. The unfolding mystery of God in Christ, of Jew and Gentile drawn together, and of the **one new man** company is now clearer. Yet, our purpose in this writing was not just to educate and inform, but also to touch your heart with revelation.

We ask you not to respond with your mind or your emotions alone. It is your spirit that we are seeking to awaken with these truths.

Will you seek God? Will you intercede? Will you invest time, effort, and resources toward the salvation of Israel? Will you labor toward the coming forth of the **one new man**? Could you enlarge your vision to include a burden that is, seemingly, not yours? It will be costly, but the rewards are clearly spelled out with God's own pen:

> **"Shall I bring to the point of birth, and not give delivery?"** says the Lord. **"Or shall I who gives delivery shut the womb?"** says our God. **"Be joyful with Jerusalem and rejoice for her, all you who love her; be exceedingly glad with her, all you who mourn over her, that you may nurse and be satisfied with her comforting breasts, that you may suck and be delighted with her bountiful bosom."** For thus says the Lord, **"Behold, I extend peace to her like a river, and the glory of the nations like an overflowing stream; and you shall be nursed, you shall be carried on the hip and fondled on the knees. As one whom his mother comforts, so I will comfort you; and you shall be comforted in Jerusalem"** (Isaiah 66:9-13).